Endorsements for Hocke

"Kevin is a mental trainer with a[n] [...] and passion for the game of hockey. He has been a hockey dad, a hockey coach and co-creator of hockeytough.com, an excellent website coaching the mental game of hockey. In *Hockey Grit, Grind, and Mind*, Kevin shares his perspective and interest in helping players develop a winning mindset."

Dr. Saul L. Miller, Sport Psychologist and Author of *Hockey Tough*

"Working with Kevin as the Head Coach and General Manager of the Sioux City Musketeers in the USHL, his mental toughness training was a huge help to our young players. The USHL is a big step, even for elite players. Kevin's work really helped our kids adapt to that transition and helped them accelerate their development throughout the year. I believe that what the guys learned about mental toughness was a contributing factor to our mid season turn around!"

Brett Larson, Assistant Men's Hockey Coach.
University of Minnesota Duluth

"The most important aspect of development and training for a hockey player is between their ears, the body follows the mind and *Hockey Grit, Grind and Mind* will guide you through that development process. A must read for today's player."

Shane Malloy, Author of *The Art of Scouting*

"Being able to transfer practice performance to game performance is a critical skill for the elite hockey player. Kevin gives you the skills and the mental toughness to be your best on game day. If you want to move up and stand out in hockey, you have to read this book"

Brent Johnson, 12 Year Veteran NHL Goalie

"Players in the NHL must be strong in both mind and body. Every player will benefit from what Kevin coaches in his book *Hockey Grit, Grind and Mind*. This is stuff that every player needs to know and is essential coaching for developing mental toughness in today's player."

Greg Smith, MS, ATC, PTA, Former NHL Athletic Trainer, Co-owner of Pivot Physical Therapy

"As a former player and coach at the Professional, College and Junior levels, I see everyday how important mental toughness is in players. Without grit and mental toughness players won't reach their full potential. *Hockey Grit, Grind, and Mind* has everything today's player needs to strengthen their mental toughness. Kevin's background and educational prowess clearly show the passion he brings to the table to not only prepare players but to help them each step of the way"

Tony McAulay, Former Pro Player and Coach, Head Coach for DeMatha Prep

"Today's game is as competitive as it has ever been and without focus and toughness, players will struggle to stay on top. *Hockey Grit Grind and Mind* is a must read if you want to stand out be able to perform under pressure. I highly recommend it"

Kevin St. Jacques, Former Pro Player and WHL Standout, Head Coach for Atlanta Jr. Knights

Hockey Grit, Grind and Mind

HOCKEY GRIT GRIND &MIND

Your Playbook for Increasing Toughness, Focus, Drive, Resilience, Confidence, and Consistency in Today's Game

Kevin L. Willis, PhD

NEW YORK

LONDON • NASHVILLE • MELBOURNE • VANCOUVER

Hockey Grit, Grind, and Mind

Your Playbook for Increasing Toughness, Focus, Drive, Resilience, Confidence, and Consistency in Today's Game

© 2019 Kevin L. Willis, PhD

Published in New York, New York, by Morgan James Publishing. Morgan James is a trademark of Morgan James, LLC. www.MorganJamesPublishing.com

The Morgan James Speakers Group can bring authors to your live event. For more information or to book an event visit The Morgan James Speakers Group at www.TheMorganJamesSpeakersGroup.com.

ISBN 9781683508304 paperback
ISBN 9781683508311 eBook
Library of Congress Control Number:2017917160

Cover Design by:
John Bleau and Rachel Lopez

Interior Illustrations by:
John Bleau

Interior Design by:
Paul Curtis

In an effort to support local communities, raise awareness and funds, Morgan James Publishing donates a percentage of all book sales for the life of each book to Habitat for Humanity Peninsula and Greater Williamsburg.

Get involved today! Visit
www.MorganJamesBuilds.com

TO, EVE, TANNER, DALLAS, AND KALEB—
THANK YOU FOR YOUR MOTIVATION, PATIENCE,
BELIEF, SUPPORT, AND LOVE.

Contents

Foreword

It used to be that players that wanted to be successful in hockey just had to worry about getting on the ice and developing their hockey skills. That's not enough anymore. In today's competitive game, players need to be a complete player. They need to have hockey skills, they need to have a high hockey IQ, and they need to be mentally tough.

As a pro player in the NHL for more than 10 years and TV hockey analyst with NBC Sports for the Washington Capitals, I get to see firsthand, every day, prospects trying to get to the show, and veterans trying to stay in the show. And I can tell you, the ones that make it and the ones that stay are the ones who are as mentally tough as they are physically tough.

Mental toughness in today's game is not optional. If a player wants to play in college or pro, they better have mental toughness skills to go along with their other hockey skills or they won't last long.

As a coach working with elite players I see far too often the toll that competitive hockey can take on a young player with dreams of playing in college and as a professional. Players that neglect their mental game risk derailing their hockey future and it's up to them to make sure that mental game training is part of their overall hockey development.

That's what I like so much about Kevin's book *Hockey Grit, Grind, and Mind*, as it captures the essence of what it means to be mentally tough in hockey and he provides a complete framework for being able to make mental toughness development part of a player's overall development. He breaks down all the core mental toughness skills that all players, from Pee Wee to Pro, need to have, to become the best player they can be.

As a player with average skill, I had to make sure I outworked, outplayed, and out-competed every player I went up against. I relied on mental toughness to make my mark, and for me, I had to learn all of it on my own. I can only imagine where I could have gone and how long I would have played if I had this kind of mental toughness coaching when I was coming up in hockey.

But you don't have to worry about that. All you have to do is read *Hockey Grit, Grind, and Mind*, and use the strategies that Kevin outlines in the book, and I promise that you will gain the mental toughness tools necessary to advance in hockey.

If you want to move up in hockey you have to be mentally tough. This book will help you do that.

Craig Laughlin
NHL Alumni
Analyst, Washington Capitals, NBCSports Washington

Introduction

Nineteen seconds to go: Johnson over to Ramsey. Yuri Lebedev checked by Ramsey. McClanahan is there, and the puck is still loose. Eleven seconds, then ten; the count is ticking down. Morrow up to Silk. Five seconds left in the game. Do you believe in miracles? YES!

That was the spark.

On February 22, 1980, twenty amateur collegiate players from the United States, with an average age of twenty-one and together for less than a year, defeated an experienced, professional, seasoned team from the Soviet Union. In fact, the Soviets were gold medal winners of the previous four Olympics and a team of veterans who had been playing together and perfecting their strategies for years.

Despite falling behind three times, this band of gritty, resilient, persistent Americans, led by Coach Herb Brooks, kept coming back time and time again. As the clock wound down, it was the Soviets who struggled in the final, scoreless ten minutes of play as the Americans held on to win, four to three.

Standing in front of my TV, watching this historic event unfold, I had tears in my eyes. Witnessing their heroic effort, grit, and never-say-die attitude set me on a course that changed my life.

How did this happen? How did a team of college players from the United States beat the best hockey team in the world? I had to know the answer.

Watching that historic moment in sports sparked a lifelong passion for the game that has led me to become a sport psychologist, certified mental-game coaching professional, and a Level 5 USA hockey coach.

Today, my passion is to understand and teach the grit the American team used to defeat a Russian hockey machine that had won back-to-back-to-back-to-back Olympic gold medals. My mission is to help you increase your grit and reach your full potential by increasing the amount of determination and resolve you have in your game.

Throughout my years coaching, I struggled to find books and articles and coaching material to teach grit to players committed to become the best they can be. That's why, as co-founder of hockeytough.com—with my mentor Dr. Saul Miller—and founder of TheCompletePlayer.com, I've developed products specifically designed to help hockey players improve their mental game, and I offer coaching workbooks, boot camps, team coaching, parent consultation, and private coaching.

As a mental-game coaching professional, I have observed hockey players for years. In all my time in this field, I've noticed one common element in all the best players who continue to move forward and achieve success; it is an essential trait they share with all the greatest players of the game. Can you guess what it is?

When I ask others, most guess talent. However, those who think size, skill, or talent separates the great players from the good are incorrect. It's not that talent doesn't matter; of course it does. The problem is that talent, on its own, is simply not enough. Certainly, talent plays an important role in the development of athletic ability; however, it is not the foundation on which greatness is built. So, what is the element that enables young athletes with modest natural ability to develop into exceptionally elite players?

The answer is *grit*: a persistent, dedicated, focused, motivated, passionate drive to be the best. Players with grit can endure when others, who may have more talent, fall short of their potential. Simply stated, grit allows hockey players to advance to an elite level. This book will teach you how to increase your performance, success, and enjoyment of the game by increasing your grit.

Now, before we get too far, I want to answer a question I am asked often: is grit the same as mental toughness? Essentially, yes, the terms go together. To be mentally tough, you need to have grit, and to be gritty, you must be mentally tough. Mental toughness is a defining quality of grit—perhaps grit's most important facet. It is the ability to perform at your best, regardless of what's going on around you, and it fuels your stamina and endurance. We will be discussing mental toughness in more detail in chapter 6. Grit, however—and all its dimensions—is the main topic we will consider together.

How to Use This Book

The book is organized to be read in order, with each concept building on the previous. Or you can use it as a reference tool, with each chapter discussing critical elements in your mental game, from performance factors to performance preparation to performance blocks.

In chapter 1, we will define *grit* and what it means to be a gritty, mentally tough player. Research shows, when it comes to determining which players move up and which players move out, grit is the best predictor of long-term success. It includes five key elements, which we'll cover in detail in this book: passion, perception, purpose, practice, and perseverance.

In chapter 2 we talk about *passion*, the spark that started you on your hockey journey. Something happened to ignite your interest and compel you to put in the long hours and endure the sometimes difficult journey to play hockey. You already know what the spark was for me. What was it for you?

Chapter 3 examines how self-*perception* plays a powerful role in your hockey career. A realistic view of self—both strengths and flaws—is essential if you hope to improve your game and increase your grit.

In chapter 4 we discuss *purpose*. Purpose provides the direction and guidance you need, not only to chart the right course but also to stay on target when adversity, obstacles, and setbacks stand in your way. If you don't know your values and goals, how will you ever succeed?

In chapter 5 we'll consider the qualities of productive *practice*. While every player understands the concept of practice, few understand what it takes to practice in a way that will maximize your development beyond that of your competitors. Not all practices are the same, so we will explain how to take your practice effort and results to a whole new level.

In chapter 6 we will discuss what it means to *persevere* when things get tough and you're not sure you can hang in there. Hockey is hard. Elite hockey is really hard. Yet, the players who persist and endure when times are tough are the players who move on. Perseverance is an essential performance factor that allows your best to shine through.

And finally, in chapter 7, we cycle back around to *passion*. The same passion that got you into hockey is the passion that keeps you there, day after day after day. When you love the game, the game loves you. Players with passion can make the impossible happen. And when you recognize and utilize this vital source of energy in your hockey journey, you can make great things happen.

After reading this book, you will know how to increase the consistency of your game, step up in pressure situations, play with more confidence, create a reserve of energy to tap into when things are tough, persevere when other players are giving up, crystalize your vision of success, and stand out on the ice in games and practices. I will give you the tools, insights, and strategies to help you train and compete like the pros. You are about to take your game—and your grit—to a whole new level.

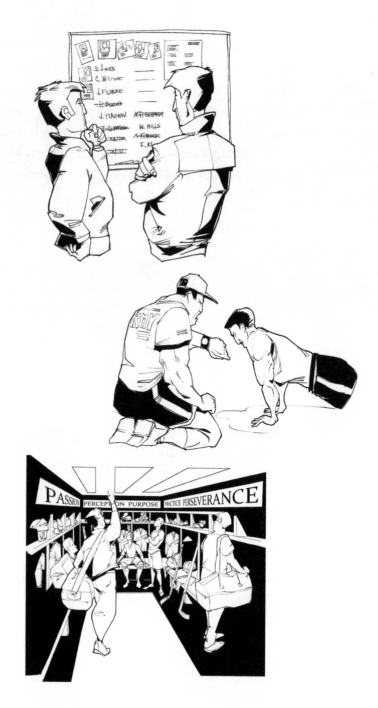

Chapter 1

What Is Grit?

It's the last day of camp and the coaches are down to their final cuts. The remaining players are equal in size, speed, skill, and experience. The front-runners for the last spot are Kyle, Tyler, and you. All appear to have what it takes to contribute to the team; unfortunately, there is only room for one more player. Who will the coaches choose?

Take a minute and picture your name on that roster sheet along with Kyle and Tyler. Think about how hard you've worked to secure a spot on a team that could do great things for your hockey future. Picture the coaches talking back and forth about all the great things you bring to the table and picture them standing at the whiteboard, getting ready to write down the name of the player who might help their team win a championship this season. What do you have that gives you the edge over the others? What will convince them to write your name on the board?

When comparing players of equal physical qualities and ability, what do coaches look for to decide which player to keep and which to let go? Grit. Grit allows a player to do whatever it takes to grow his skills and endure the long, hard climb to the elite hockey level. Without grit, there is little motivation to "push through the wall." Without grit, there is no drive to do difficult things or endure the painful training necessary to play at the highest levels.

My Grit Formula

Grit is the precursor to reaching extraordinary heights in all areas of life. It is the foundation on which greatness is built. Without it, we would not have inspiring works of art, great works of literature, brilliant inventions, or memorable moments in sports to enrich our lives. So, how do we produce grit? Is there a recipe to follow?

After coaching and consulting for years, I've compiled a list of characteristics present in players with grit—my grit formula, if you will: burning passion, accurate self-perception, resolute purpose, deliberate practice, and unwavering perseverance. To weather the ups and downs of hockey and pursue your goals, you must grow and expand in these five areas. In fact, the presence or absence of each of these "P's" determines an individual's level of grit.

Grit Research

For the past decade, grit has been the subject of much research. In fact, everything you learn in this book is based on scientific evidence that proves grit is necessary for lasting achievement. Recent research by the intelligent and gritty researcher Dr. Angela Duckworth has shined a spotlight on this mental skill and pinpointed techniques for increasing the amount of grit you possess.

Before becoming a world-renowned researcher, Dr. Duckworth taught middle school math and noticed something very interesting about her students. She examined the grades from all her students and saw there was no correlation between grades and student IQ. She found that some of her smartest students had poor grades, and some of her weaker students had high grades. Curious, she started looking at their habits and saw that some of her less academically inclined students were doing something her smartest kids were not: they were putting an extra amount of effort into their studies—not a ridiculous amount of extra study, but a deliberately increased effort.

They were going above and beyond what was expected, and, over time, their grades improved dramatically. During this same time, her smartest and most talented students did only what was asked, and even though they had a high IQ, they underperformed. It seemed the smartest kids depended on  their raw talent and high intelligence to get by, and their lower grades reflected their minimal effort.

Dr. Duckworth was driven to discover why this was happening and wondered if this same principle applied to other situations. After getting her PhD, Dr. Duckworth looked into peak performance and studied the young cadets at West Point, one of the toughest military schools in the United States. Every year, approximately 1,400 cadets are selected out of a pool of 14,000 applicants to begin training at West Point.

As with all military training, the early days are the toughest. At West Point, cadets endure weeks of brutal training known as "Beast Barracks." Researchers who have studied West Point cadets refer to Beast Barracks as an intense period of training deliberately engineered to test the very limits of cadets' physical, emotional, and mental capacities.

As you can imagine, not every cadet makes it through Beast Barracks. Statistics show that only one in five cadets will make it past the first seven weeks of training. This is somewhat surprising as getting into West Point means you beat out 12,600 other applicants, clearly indicating you are one of the best of the best. These numbers prove just how tough the training must be.

Being ever curious, Dr. Duckworth set out to understand why some cadets can endure this intense training while others fail. She looked at all aspects of performance, education, fitness, IQ, discipline, and genetics. She drilled down on high school rankings and considered the SAT, Leadership Potential, Physical Aptitude Test, and Grit Scale scores of over 2,400 cadets.

Here's what she discovered. It wasn't the cadets' physical makeup, education, leadership potential, talent, IQ, or genetics that accurately predicted the outcome of Beast Barracks. It was their grit.[1] The level of passion and perseverance to work toward long-term goals made the difference between those who made it and those who did not.

The Grit Scale

To measure grit, Dr. Duckworth developed a Grit Scale, a quick and easy assessment to measure the level of grit an individual has.[2] The remainder of this book will break down each component of grit to understand how to improve yours. So, before we can go any further, take the Grit Scale assessment so you will know your score as we work our way through the rest of this book.

There are two ways to take the Grit Scale assessment: online or manually. To take the assessment online for free, go to GritGrindMind.net. The nice thing about taking the assessment online is that it's automatically scored for you. It will take you less than five minutes to find out your score. Or, if you would rather score your assessment yourself or aren't near a computer, I've included Dr. Duckworth's eight-point Grit Scale below, which is a little different than the online version but the scores work out the same. Either way, the assessment is quick and easy, and the results are highly predictive of a person's ability to achieve under challenging circumstances.

Before you take the test, understand that your score on the Grit Scale is not static. Nor is it indicative of your level of grit in all aspects of your life. A low Grit Score does not limit your hockey potential, nor does a high Grit Score assure you of hockey success. The point of understanding grit is to understand what makes up grit and how to increase yours. I hope to provide you the tools and guidance for how to use grit as another weapon in your hockey arsenal.

Are you ready to find out how gritty you are?

Grit Scale Assessment

While considering your hockey game, please respond to the following eight items. Be honest. There are no right or wrong answers.

1. New ideas and projects sometimes distract me from previous ones.
    O Very much like me
    O Mostly like me
    O Somewhat like me
    O Not much like me
    O Not like me at all

2. Setbacks don't discourage me. I don't give up easily.
    O Very much like me
    O Mostly like me
    O Somewhat like me
    O Not much like me
    O Not like me at all

3. I have been obsessed with a certain idea or project for a short time but later lost interest.
    O Very much like me
    O Mostly like me
    O Somewhat like me
    O Not much like me
    O Not like me at all

4. I am a hard worker.
    O Very much like me
    O Mostly like me
    O Somewhat like me
    O Not much like me
    O Not like me at all

5. I often set a goal but later choose to pursue a different one.
   - ⭘ Very much like me
   - ⭘ Mostly like me
   - ⭘ Somewhat like me
   - ⭘ Not much like me
   - ⭘ Not like me at all
6. I have difficulty maintaining my focus on projects that take more than a few months to complete.
   - ⭘ Very much like me
   - ⭘ Mostly like me
   - ⭘ Somewhat like me
   - ⭘ Not much like me
   - ⭘ Not like me at all
7. I finish whatever I begin.
   - ⭘ Very much like me
   - ⭘ Mostly like me
   - ⭘ Somewhat like me
   - ⭘ Not much like me
   - ⭘ Not like me at all
8. I am diligent. I never give up.
   - ⭘ Very much like me
   - ⭘ Mostly like me
   - ⭘ Somewhat like me
   - ⭘ Not much like me
   - ⭘ Not like me at all

Scoring

For questions 2, 4, 7, and 8, assign the following points:

5 = Very much like me

4 = Mostly like me

3 = Somewhat like me

2 = Not much like me

1 = Not like me at all

For questions 1, 3, 5, and 6, assign the following points:

1 = Very much like me

2 = Mostly like me

3 = Somewhat like me

4 = Not much like me

5 = Not like me at all

Add up all the points and divide by eight. The maximum score on this scale is five (extremely gritty), and the lowest score is one (not at all gritty).

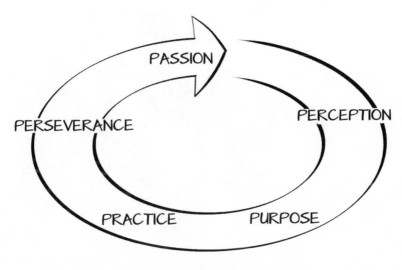

The grit cycle

Now that you have a better understanding of grit and even know your Grit Score, let's break down each of the factors that make up grit: passion, self-perception, purpose, practice, and perseverance. Each element leads to the next: passion flows into self-perception, which is necessary to understand your purpose, which inspires practice, which requires perseverance, which flows back to passion—and the cycle continues.

So, let's get started with the element that put you on this hockey journey in the first place: passion.

Chapter 2

Passion to Start

Arguably the greatest basketball player of all time, Michael Jordan had such passion for the game that he had a "love of the game" clause built into his contract with the Chicago Bulls. While most NBA organizations prevent their athletes from participating in unsanctioned games, such as pickup ball or street ball, Michael Jordan had such an abiding passion and dedication for basketball that he insisted on being able to play wherever and whenever he wanted. It is a passion that led Michael Jordan to achieve the highest level of performance, leading to five MVP awards, ten scoring titles, and the Chicago Bulls' "three-peat" as NBA champions in the 1990s.

You may not realize it, but Jordan wasn't so successful his first time out. As a sophomore in high school, the then 5'11" Jordan was deemed too short for the varsity team, so his coach placed him on the JV team. This placement motivated young Jordan to prove his value in the game, and he launched into an intense period of practice that led to tremendous growth in skill. That season, Jordan went on to lead the JV team, chalking up several forty-plus point games, and he never looked back.

Michael Jordan's story illustrates just how important passion is. If Jordan didn't have a burning passion for basketball, he would not have worked so hard his sophomore year to improve his skills, and his career may have ended before it even started. Quite simply, his love for the game drove him to develop his talents and set him on a course to change the game.

Passion in hockey is multifaceted. It's both the spark that sets things in motion and the fire that keeps things moving forward. In this chapter,

we're going to focus on that first spark, the passion for hockey that got you started in the game. We will also explore three fundamental questions you must answer if you are determined to increase your grit: What do you really want out of hockey? What do you truly believe about yourself? What are you willing to do? Passion will underpin and inform your answers to these questions as it is the motivating force for all you do.

The 1980 men's Olympic hockey team put me on the path to becoming an expert in mental toughness. We don't always know when and where this spark will happen, but you will know it when it happens. I grew up playing baseball, soccer, and football, but watching that epic, miraculous moment in 1980 changed me forever. My passion for hockey was ignited right then and there and has been burning brightly ever since.

Ignition

The decision to pursue and develop any talent will typically come from some sort of igniting factor. Similar to my spark story, the 1980 US men's hockey team's "Miracle on Ice" also motivated many great American-born players to aim for the NHL. Players like Mike Modano, Pat LaFontaine, Jeremy Roenick, Ed Olczyk, Bobby Carpenter, Mike Richter, Tom Barrasso, Joe Mullen, Brian Leetch, Chris Chelios, and others point to this moment in history as the driving force behind their passion for the game. Other ignition sources include parental encouragement, solid coaching, natural talent, or a powerful interest in learning how to do something well. Whatever the source, the spark is what lights the fire that ultimately drives your passion to become the best you can be.

The original flash point of ignition is usually unexpected and can feel like a revelation or something that was "meant to be." Pursuit of this new, exciting skill or ability usually creates such joy that the hard work and difficulty surrounding advancement becomes fuel to work even harder, not reason to give up. This is a very important point regarding the development of your talent in hockey. The stronger your passion and drive for hockey, the more likely you will hang in there when progress means sacrifice.

I'm sure many of you have experienced a spark like this and know exactly what I'm talking about. Think back to a time where you did something or saw something that instantly motivated you to find out more. It feels incredible when you discover something so amazing that it's all you can think of and all you want to do. It's this kind of spark that ignites the passion needed to play hockey at the highest levels.

Look at some of the best players in the game today, guys like Crosby, Ovechkin, Toews, Kane, Matthews, and McDavid. What makes these guys willing to log tedious hours working on the small and seemingly insignificant parts of the game, which ultimately make a huge difference in their performance? These players work hard because they know the answers to three fundamental questions pertaining to passion:

1. What do you want?
2. What do you believe?
3. What are you willing to do?

What Do You Really Want?

What do you want out of hockey? Your answer matters because your passion is driven by what you want and what you believe is possible.

Like most players, I'm sure you've watched games on television and thought to yourself, *I want that. I want to be able to play hockey*

like those guys. I remember going to my first hockey game and being absolutely amazed at how intense and exciting it was. I grew up watching players like Gretzky and Lemieux dazzle hockey fans with their skill and scoring finesse. Watching my heroes on the ice fueled the fire that burns to this day.

The first step to understanding the passion you have for hockey is to remember what drew you to the game and define what you want to experience as a player. Knowing what you want is essential, but there is more. You must also believe you have what it takes to reach the dream you so desperately want.

What Do You Believe?

Do you genuinely believe you will do whatever it takes to succeed? Do you believe you can develop your talent to play at the highest levels, or do you sometimes doubt you have what it takes to remain true to your dream and work hard?

Belief in yourself is paramount to your success. Negative beliefs, even those unconsciously held, become self-limiting. Bill Gates is a billionaire because he believed there was nothing holding him back from building the largest and most profitable software company in the world. Peyton Manning is one of the most  successful quarterbacks of all time because of his unfailing belief in his ability to succeed in football. Sidney Crosby will find himself in the Hall of Fame one day because he knew that with the right focus, the right attitude, and the necessary commitment to his game, he would be a star.

How about you? What do you believe about yourself? Answer the following questions as they relate to hockey:

1. Do you believe that success in hockey is a choice you make every time you step on the ice?
2. Do you believe you can do what it takes to develop your skills and talent as a hockey player?
3. Can you truly see yourself moving forward to higher and more elite levels in hockey?
4. Do you believe talent is not inherited but can grow and develop with the right kind of coaching and personal effort?
5. Do you believe you deserve to be successful in hockey?
6. Do you believe you have all the available resources necessary to succeed?

When I talk about resources, I'm talking about elite coaching, quality hockey facilities, support from family and friends, and guidance from trusted professionals and advisors. Are you playing in competitive leagues against competitive teams? Are you getting opportunities to be scouted at tournaments and showcases?

Belief is a tricky thing because each of us can harbor secret doubts that we have not even admitted to ourselves. By paying attention to your internal dialog, you may notice negative self-talk, which indicates a lack of belief in one or more parts of your game. In the moment you catch yourself lacking belief, choose to face the doubt head-on and lean into the struggle. Remember, we choose what we believe just as surely as we choose what we say, how we behave, how we react to adversity, and what we think and feel. Belief is a choice, and if your beliefs limit you, it's time to face them and change them.

What Are You Willing to Do?

As you begin to clarify what you want and peel back the layers of what you believe about yourself, it's time to decide what you are willing to do for the sake of your passion. Consider the following questions and be honest with yourself about the answers:

1. Can I clearly see, in my mind's eye, what I want out of hockey?
2. Am I dedicated to mastering the skills necessary to become the player I want to be?
3. Am I willing to put in the kind of work it will take to achieve all I have set out to accomplish?
4. Am I willing to work hard and make the necessary sacrifices to achieve an elite level?

NOTE: This exercise can be used to examine other areas of your life as well. Whether it's school, work, friends, or other pursuits, knowing what you want, what you believe is possible, and what you're willing to do puts you on the path to success.

The bottom line is this: passion for what you want, a belief you have what it takes, and a willingness to do the work is the foundation for becoming an elite hockey player.

We see now that a simple spark of passion gave us all the dream of achieving hockey greatness, but self-perception also plays a role in how far we'll go. In the next chapter, we'll explore, in depth, what makes you as a player unique. By understanding and maximizing your specific traits, you can formulate a plan to accomplish your goals and achieve your vision.

Chapter 3

Perception

Though it is easy to forget, you bring something unique to hockey, a story and set of skills that are your very own. You are unlike any other player in your particular strengths, weaknesses, and struggles. We are all working toward the same goal: becoming an elite player. But, depending on where you are right now with skill and drive, the path to greatness will vary.

Perception—or more accurately, self-perception—looks beyond actions to the attitudes that motivate the action. It requires insight and discernment and will ultimately produce in you an appreciation of how you are wired. As we are just beginning our journey together, it seems an appropriate time to stop and take stock of all you have to offer and all you need to improve. In short, an honest self-assessment is the first step to becoming a fierce, gritty competitor. This chapter will enrich your self-awareness, making you more conscious of your personal expectations and motivation. There will be an opportunity for you to complete formal personality assessments and reevaluate destructive thoughts that threaten to undermine your confidence and growth.

Become Self-Aware

Personal awareness is the first step in making any positive change in your life. You can't change what you don't recognize in yourself. To add grit to your game, you must first be keenly aware of the areas of your game that need shoring up. What do you need to change, add, or develop to grow an unstoppable dedication to hockey?

Honesty

Although it isn't always easy to assess yourself, it is always rewarding. Self-assessment leads to self-awareness. And self-awareness can be the impetus for lasting and positive change in your life and your game. Honesty is essential. You don't want to be overly critical, nor do you want to be overly complimentary. Try to see your "real" self so that you can grow into your "ideal" self. Honest self-assessment is the first step in reaching your true potential as an athlete.

Checking In

We all operate at different levels of self-awareness. Our level of self-awareness changes depending on the situation—in some areas we are more self-aware than in others. Learning how to "check in" with your emotional self, regardless of the situation, is a critical skill in developing grit. There are four basic levels of self-awareness, ranging from least aware to most aware:

- **Level IV:** Unconscious. Our unconscious includes what we don't really know—and may not want to know. What we know in our unconscious is trapped in the recesses of our mind and is typically stored there instinctively as a protective mechanism.

- **Level III:** Subconscious. This part of our being lies just below the surface of awareness and involves learned patterns and feelings that we haven't taken time to examine or process.
- **Level II:** Conscious. This is the part of the self we are aware of on a day-to-day basis.
- **Level I:** Consciously Conscious. This is the self-knowledge you know that you know. Achieving this level of awareness is pivotal in increasing grit.

Formal Assessments

If you are a member of TheCompletePlayer.com or hockeytough.com (sign up for free at GritGrindMind.net), you have access to the player assessment tools we use with players to help them understand their current player personality profile. These assessments can shed light on your habits and tendencies as a player. They can help you make sense of why you do what you do, why you think the way you think, and why you feel what you feel.

Much of what we will talk about will assume you have a clear understanding about yourself as a player: your emotions, your feelings, what you're thinking, and what you want. But let's face it; that is not always the case. A lot of times that level of clarity just isn't there. We feel like we know what we want and where we're going, but then we do something foolish and end up off course. Why do we do things that get in our own way? It comes down to knowing yourself.

The assessments I prefer to use with players are the Complete Player Profile, the Grit Scale, the HockeyType assessment, and the Test of Attentional and Interpersonal Style, known as TAIS. This last tool is the one I use most often. Take time to visit the Complete Player website to complete each now. To find a link to these assessments, go to GritGrindMind.net.

The Complete Player Profile

The Complete Player Profile is a three-part assessment that provides instant feedback on player strengths and personality style, and it highlights opportunities for growth and improvement. It looks at areas such as confidence, focus, competitiveness, grit, doubt, social approval, and expectations and offers feedback and strategies for improvement in all of these mental skill areas.

Grit Scale Assessment

As we discussed at the beginning of the book, the Grit Scale is a quick assessment that reveals the special blend of passion and persistence a player has in the pursuit of his goals. If you don't know your Grit Score, be sure to go back and take this assessment. It's free, and your score is one of the most important numbers to know.

HockeyType Assessment

The HockeyType assessment is an assessment tool adapted from the Fisher Temperament Inventory by Dr. Helen Fisher. It offers insight into your biologically based personality traits to understand how those traits influence you as a player or a coach. Knowing your HockeyType can give you a better understanding of what causes you to think, act, and feel the way you do.

One of the fun things I did with this assessment on my website is to match the different temperaments described by the test with those of superheroes. Are you more like Ironman or Batman? How about Captain America or Spiderman?

The assessment is free, and it's a great way to dip your toe in the water with player assessment tools and start to learn a little more about the way your brain works.

TAIS Assessment

TAIS is a proven and highly recommended sport assessment tool that has been around since the late 1970s. Developed by Dr. Robert Nideffer, the TAIS assessment[3]—more than any other inventory available today—provides the information needed for performance prediction, athlete selection, performance enhancement, and team building in situations where people must perform at extremely high levels and/or when individuals are under a great deal of pressure to perform. TAIS helps players and coaches answer these questions:[4]

1. Are you able to consistently perform at a high level while under pressure and when everything is on the line?
2. Are certain situations and conditions more likely to lead to success or failure for you? What are those situations and conditions?
3. What can you do in your development to make sure you get the most out of your skill when it really counts?
4. Are you able and willing to do the work and make the changes required to be more successful in hockey?

How Aware Are You?

Now, take a look at your results. Are there areas where your score was higher than you thought it would be? How about lower? It is time to be honest with yourself and to ask others to be honest with you. As you consider self-assessment and self-awareness, be open and willing to learn and grow.

I talk a lot about self-assessment with the players I work with; you can't fix what you don't acknowledge. As human beings, it is very difficult to step back and objectively evaluate our own skill level and recognize our deficiencies, but improvement starts by knowing what you need to work on and knowing how to work on it.

Feedback is critical for improvement; however, I say that with one very important distinction. Professional or experienced feedback is important, not just any feedback. Professional or experienced feedback is what I define as reliable, trustworthy feedback from someone who knows the sport. While we love it when Mom and Dad come to our games, their feedback is—well, let's say it may not be as unbiased and appropriate as your coach's. It's not that their feedback is wrong or out of line, it just may not be the best information to use when making adjustments to your game.

Evaluate Personal Expectations

I want to take a minute and talk about an area in every player's mental game that can have a powerful impact on development and performance. This impact can be either positive or negative, depending on how you manage this critical mental skill.

I'm talking about personal expectations, which are unique for each individual. Expectations are simple predictions of what you think is going to happen (usually based on what has happened in the past). Understanding the expectations you hold for yourself is a critical part of self-perception because the specific expectations you have for the future can dramatically influence the level of effort you give, the risks you take, and the investment you are willing to make in hockey. In short, your passion and drive—your grit—will be affected by your expectations. It's important to set healthy expectations that will keep you working toward your goals. Here are a few truths to keep in mind as we talk about your expectations for your future in hockey:

- Expectations can range from low to normal to high to unrealistic.
- Expectations have a direct impact on your confidence and performance.
- Expectations come from both internal and external sources—meaning you have expectations about yourself as a player and others (coaches, parents, peers) have expectations about you as well.
- Expectations are good (if they help you) or bad (if they interfere with your performance).

Types of Expectations

Your personal expectations can be *great expectations*, which will stretch you to perform your best and aid your development. Or they can be *self-limiting expectations*, which put pressure on you and hurt your performance. Expectations can also range from low to normal to high to unrealistic. It's important to be aware of the various types of expectations and the effect they can have on your game.

High Expectations

High expectations are what help good players become great. They allow players to stretch and expand their skills and reach beyond their typical levels of performance to elite levels of performance. High expectations form when players show budding signs of excellence but are unable to sustain it for any length of time.

During these fleeting moments, your true potential shines through, and expectations are raised as you envision what you can truly accomplish. Self-confidence grows as you then strive to reach these new levels again and again. Your expectations are real because you were just there, albeit for a brief time, but it happened. You felt it. It's possible, and you liked it.

Once you get a taste of that increased performance level, you'll get hungry for it again and again. This is where grit can help. With intense drive and focus, you'll work harder in practice. You'll endure and spend more time working to expand your skills. You'll begin to believe that what you thought was possible is, in fact, very possible. I call this "lighting the fire." Once you feel the spark, it's up to you to fan the flames to keep it going.

Properly understood and managed, high expectations are where good players become great players. One word of caution, however. While high expectations have the potential to create elite players and top teams, they are also a double-edged sword and can cause great frustration if they begin to stray into the area of unrealistic expectations.

Self-Limiting Expectations

Remember, self-limiting expectations are those that are too low or unrealistic. *Low expectations* occur when we expect very little from ourselves. With low expectations, very little effort is given, which results in a poor performance. With little to gain, low expectations lead players to put in little effort or give up altogether, as they figure it isn't worth the effort.

Unrealistic expectations are devious and damaging mental errors that must be identified and eliminated at all costs. Unrealistic expectations are expectations that are not supported by any evidence and sometimes not even grounded in reality. Unrealistic expectations can take players with great futures and unlimited potential and burn them out before they ever reach their greatness.

Unrealistic expectations, whether internal or external, are the single greatest cause of burnout in hockey. What makes them so devious is that it's sometimes hard to tell them apart from high expectations. The best method I know to separate high expectations from unrealistic expectations is to determine if the expected outcome has ever happened before (to anyone) or has ever happened to someone like you—your age, size, skill level, and playing circumstances, etc. Once you're honest about whether the hoped-for outcome is possible, then you can gauge how much of a stretch it will require and if that stretch is possible without breaking you.

Do You Have Smart Expectations?

Are you managing your expectations, or are your expectations managing you? Consider the following precepts:

- **Expectations are designed to stretch you, not break you.** Do not allow expectations to become strict rules that stress you out if you don't meet them. Falling short of expectations should fire you up, not tear you down.
- **Do not critically judge your skills and performance based on expectations.** Rather, *evaluate* your performance based on your expectation and adjust as needed. Remember, expectations are designed to lift you up, not push you down.
- **When expectations cause stress and frustration, they are either too high or unrealistic; change something!** Stress and frustration inhibit development and hurt performance. Review your expectations and make sure they are helping you grow, not holding you back.
- **If you find yourself losing the fun in hockey, it might be because of poorly managed expectations.** Meeting and exceeding expectations should produce joy and excitement. If all you feel is relief when meeting your expectations, then it's time to change something. Don't let overly high expectations steal the joy and satisfaction from personal and team success.

I worked with a U16 team who experienced how expectations can affect enjoyment of the game. Let's call them the Sharks.

The Sharks were a highly ranked team and the favorite heading into the championship tournament. Playing well in the playoffs, they were seeded as the first-place team in the semifinals and would have to go against the team seeded fourth.

Throughout the game, both teams played well. The Sharks got off to a quick start and scored two goals in the first period. The Bears came back in the second period to get two goals of their own. Heading into the third period, it was tied up until the Bears got a lucky bounce off the end boards and were able to jam the puck home to take the lead. Caught a little off guard by the unexpected goal, the Sharks were slow off the faceoff, and the Bears quickly scored again to go up by two goals with only five minutes to play in the third.

As the tournament favorite, the Sharks had their hands full. For the next four minutes, the teams traded chances. With one minute left in the game, the Sharks turned up the heat and connected for a goal to get within one.

With the clock winding down, the Sharks played brilliantly and scored another goal to tie it. With ten seconds left to play, the Sharks tilted the ice, and with the Bears reeling in their own end, the Sharks

scored the game winner right as the horn sounded. They did it. The Sharks were going on to the finals.

Okay, so here's my question: how did the players feel after that amazing comeback against a team they probably should have beaten easily? Well, I can tell you. In addition to being exhausted at the end of the game, most of the players were disappointed. They were disappointed because they almost lost. In their minds, that game should have been a breeze; instead, without their amazing comeback, they would've gone home.

But they won. They were going on to the finals. They should've been flying high. This illustrates how expectations can steal the joy from something that should otherwise leave you elated. I'm sure many of you can identify with this example, so I challenge you to remember this section of the book. If you're ever in a game like that and you do the impossible, I want you to be over the moon and proud of your accomplishment. If you find yourself experiencing more frustration than joy, evaluate your expectations.

Expectations and Performance

There is a clear and well-documented connection between expectations and performance. When you believe in your ability and have confidence, you will try harder and stay at it longer, thus increasing your chances of success. This kind of determination is a key component in grit. If, however, you've had limited success, you'll go into the situation expecting very little and ultimately achieve exactly that—very little.

Expectations are one reason the best players in the world are the best players in the world. But they're also the reason why some great players, with all the potential in the world, never made it out of junior hockey.

Think about it. When you've had success in the past, you believed your efforts would pay off so you were willing to do more and work harder to accomplish your mission and achieve your goals.

Understanding expectations, and how they affect your performance, is a key mental skill when it comes to improving the amount of grit you have in your game. There is a direct link between how good you are and how good you think you should be. Your skill as a player is affected by how you expect to play or how you think others expect you to play.

When you believe (expect) that you can be successful playing elite hockey, you will work harder and persist longer when faced with obstacles and difficulties. Your expectations are backed by the evidence of your past successes; thus, you are encouraged to make ongoing investments of time, effort, and resources that pay off in improved performance.

Players with low expectations are easily discouraged and wilt in the face of adversity and difficulty. They have little to no interest in investing the time and effort necessary to play at a higher level; thus, their performance and motivation die on the vine.

External Expectations

Expectations from others will often increase the expectations players have for themselves. Two players of equal skill and ability placed on two different teams can have dramatic differences in development, depending on the level of expectation within each group. Called the Pygmalion Effect, when players are placed in groups with either high or low expectations, the players will almost always meet the expectations held for the group, regardless of their individual skill, ability, or potential.

External expectations can have positive or negative effects on players—especially if the consequences of those expectations are not understood, managed, and in alignment with the expectations the players have for themselves. It is common to see high expectations imposed by others as a source of stress and anxiety on players. On the other hand, sometimes by helping players raise their expectations and pushing the envelope on their perceived skills and capabilities, a coach can find a passion and ability in the player that would have otherwise gone undiscovered. Finding that line between normal and high expectations and knowing how hard to push is a skill and an art for coaches and parents.

Examine Motivation

Of all of the factors that affect grit, motivation is one of the most important. Your motivation to succeed is a top predictor of how successful you will be as a hockey player.

Again, self-awareness is crucial. If you took the Complete Player Profile assessment or TAIS assessment on TheCompletePlayer.com, take a look at your assessment scores for motivation. How did you do? If you have a low score in this area, ask yourself the following questions. These are honest questions I hear from players every day:

1. Is my motivation low because I am worried about making mistakes or playing poorly?
2. Is my motivation low because I am trying to protect my ego?
3. Is my motivation low because I'm burned out or hockey just isn't fun anymore?
4. Is my motivation low because I am under so much pressure from outside influences—coaches, parents, or teammates—that it's interfering with my play?
5. Is my motivation low because I've been training hard but don't feel like I'm getting better or going anywhere?

If your motivation is low, find out why. Once you identify the reasons, you can determine the best course of action to rediscover the motivation you once had for pursuing the sport. Remember, girt requires hard work and stamina—both of which are impossible without the inner drive motivation brings.

How Motivated Are You?

When I work with players and evaluate their drive, I often see three common motivational tendencies. The first tendency is the overmotivated player, the player who is passionate and driven, almost to the point of obsession. The second tendency I see is the undermotivated player; these players struggle to stay pumped, committed, or driven to do the work necessary to play at the level they say they want to play at. The third type is the balanced player, whose motivation is a balance between the two. In becoming a Complete Player, it is important for you to understand where your motivation comes from and learn to balance your drive so that you can enjoy the benefits of being driven, motivated, and committed, without going overboard and becoming fanatical, perfectionistic, or stressed out.

Most of the players I work with lean toward being overmotivated, rather than undermotivated, but believe it or not, there are good and bad points for each. Players in the overmotivated category have a high level of intensity, a strong work ethic, and an intense desire to succeed; however, despite this high motivation, they can sometimes underachieve because they feel the need to be perfect. These players struggle with anxiety or fear of failing because succeeding in hockey is so important to them.

The following chart presents a list of tendencies for both the overmotivated and undermotivated player. As you read these characteristics, notice how there are both positive and negative aspects in both columns. Ask yourself which tendencies sound more like you. Remember, the goal is to find a balance between the two.

Tendencies for the Over- and Undermotivated Player

Overmotivated Player Tendencies	Undermotivated Player Tendencies
• has trouble trusting self in competition	• performs well in competition
• highly motivated with strong work ethic	• appears lazy and unconcerned about performance
• fears failure and is afraid to make mistakes	
• low level of self-confidence	• highly confident in ability, with solid trust on game day
• has a perfectionist attitude—overly critical of self	• believes skill and success are determined by natural-born talent
• willing to work on weaknesses	• doesn't believe effort and persistence are critical for success
• doesn't believe it's possible to work too hard	
• with failure, blames self for not working hard enough	• doesn't feel the burning need to work hard to improve
• responds to mistakes by overanalyzing and being overly critical	• early advantage in skills and confidence undermines motivation
• craves praise for working hard	• made to feel guilty for not appearing to love hockey or take it seriously
• approval from others is extremely important	
• easily becomes frustrated and discouraged in the face of failure	• passive, laid-back, nonjudgmental, and relaxed personality
• responds to failure by working harder	• appears to lack motivation in practice and games
• constantly works on technique	
• replays mistakes over and over in his mind	• becomes frustrated with teammates with less skill and doesn't understand why they can't play better
• wants others to see him as having a great attitude in pressure situations	
• is prone to becoming analytical and overcontrolling	• remembers successes and great plays, rather than mistakes or bad games
• tries to "think" his way through a game	• in pressure situations, trusts his skills, relies on instincts, and goes with the flow

Overmotivated Players

So, after reading through the list, did you see characteristics of the overmotivated player in yourself? If you are more of the overmotivated player type, then your drive is dialed up pretty high and you probably compete hard in everything you do. You most likely have a strong work ethic and know hard work alone isn't enough to guarantee success. The biggest struggle with overmotivated players is their desire to be perfect and their worry that, even after all the hard work they've put in, they might still come up short. This fear of failure can create stress and anxiety, which can lead to performance issues when things aren't going well. Below is a list of advantages and disadvantages of overmotivated players.

Overmotivated Players: The Good

- They have learned to work hard for everything they have, which has reinforced the importance of drive, passion, and persistence in hockey.
- Their hard work paid off, allowing them to stand out at an early age.
- They have a great deal of pride in how hard they work.
- They're very passionate and dedicated to their hockey development.
- Coaches love them because they are such hard workers in both practices and games and are a great example for other players to follow.

Overmotivated Players: The Bad

Although early life experience resulted in drive and motivation, that drive doesn't always translate into a sense of confidence.

Sometimes it is this lack of confidence or belief in their abilities that drives them to work so hard.

- They feel the need to be perfect and mistake-free in practice and games.
- Doubt in their abilities can cause them to play too carefully to avoid making any mistakes.
- They can be overly analytical and judgmental about their performance.
- They spend a lot of time thinking about what just happened or what might happen and find it hard to stay in the moment.
- They worry too much about what others think and let that concern affect their play.
- They downplay the good things they do.
- They find it difficult to dial it back, chill out, and have fun.
- Their excessive desire to get better can lead to frustration and burnout.

Strategies for the Overmotivated Player

- Have a long memory for success and a short memory for failure. You can learn from failure, certainly. Take a look at your poor performances and learn from them. Then move on. Enjoy your successes and remember them when visualizing how you want to play.
- Set realistic goals and make sure the expectations you have for your play are grounded in reality. Set goals that make you better as a hockey player, rather than setting goals that are purely about winning.
- Learn to let go of perceived pressure from others, including worrying about what they are thinking or saying about you. Recognize that most of this is just inside your head. As I've said to many players I work with, "You're so worried about what others are thinking

about you. If you found out how little they actually do think about you, you'd probably be insulted."

Undermotivated Players

So, what about the undermotivated player? At first glance, you might think there's no real advantage to being an undermotivated player, but one of the things I find with undermotivated players is they tend to be naturally skilled players with lots of raw talent. They're usually bigger, stronger players, and they play with confidence and trust their game. However, it's because they are, and have been, such a good player over the years that they've missed out on learning what it takes to bear down when things are tough. After all, why work so hard and be so driven if you're having success already? Grit seems less critical to them.

Well, it would be great to think you will always have a skill or physical advantage over others. But what happens when things stop being so easy? Will you be able to dig deep to succeed if you've never learned how to work hard? It is essential, if you are undermotivated, to find ways to challenge yourself and strive for improvement. Below, I list the advantages and disadvantages for this player type.

Undermotivated Players: The Good

- They are usually talented at an early age and may have been gifted with size.
- Their success in hockey came early and often.
- They probably didn't have to work as hard or put in the same amount of effort as others to stand out and play well.
- Their advanced skill and early success gave them a sense of high self-esteem.
- They are usually able to stay loose and play relaxed during games.

- They seem to be able to play "in the zone" more often.
- Coaches love their positive, relaxed attitude and the confidence with which they play.

Undermotivated Players: The Bad

- Their early talent and confidence can undermine their ability to develop drive and motivation.
- Sometimes they feel like working hard isn't all that important—as long as they have the talent to back it up.
- Sometimes they can come off as undedicated or dispassionate about hockey to their teammates and coach.
- Sometimes they can be seen by others as skilled but lazy.
- They may struggle to bear down or stay motivated when things get tough.
- Their compete level is inconsistent and sometimes on the low side, causing them to struggle with grit and determination.
- They can be frustrating to play with because they just don't seem to be intense or engaged.

Strategies for the Undermotivated Player

- Be willing to recognize personal weaknesses and look for opportunities to improve. Pick several areas in your game where you'd like to improve and set goals to become better in those areas.
- Have a plan. It may be that you've had the ability to coast on your natural skills, but do you really want to waste your raw potential? Think about how good you could become with a little more drive in your game. Sit down with your coaches and find out where they think

your game can go. Set goals and go on a mission to become a better player.

- Bring it in practice like you bring it on game day. Challenge yourself in practices to strengthen your weaknesses and develop new skills. Set the bar high for yourself to see just how good you can be.

- Remember back to the reasons you started playing hockey in the first place. Find ways to reignite your passion for the game and use it as fuel to increase your overall drive.

Balance

Ideally, your hockey drive is a balance of the best parts of the overmotivated and undermotivated player type. The goal is to find areas of your game where you are undermotivated and use the strategies we talked about to strengthen your work ethic and compete level. If you are overmotivated, use the strategies mentioned to feed your passion and commitment to hockey, but balance it with trust and confidence. Then, you can get the most out of your abilities on game day.

Sources of Motivation

When you boil it down, there are really two sources of motivation. The first source of motivation is internal motivation, and it comes from inside you (your passion, your commitment, your goals). The other source of motivation comes from external sources, things outside of you (attention, playing time, recognition, appreciation, acceptance). It is important to recognize both sources of motivation, and it is also important to recognize the control you have over each.

Internally motivated players have a fire in their belly to compete and be the best. They love the game; they love to battle; and they love to win. Their inner drive fuels their goals, their effort, and their passion.

Players who are motivated internally have a burning desire to succeed in everything they do. They don't hold back, and they play with optimistic confidence. Grit is often apparent in these players as endurance and hard work are fueled by their inner drive.

Externally motivated players depend more on external rewards for their motivation. Things like attention, compliments, recognition, and acceptance are important reasons they play hockey, and without some of these factors, hockey just wouldn't be as important. Because external rewards are the primary source of their motivation, these players are at risk of losing motivation if they don't get positive feedback to drive them. When there is a dip in external recognition, they can lose their drive and find it difficult to stay pumped on a consistent basis. These players may struggle with developing grit as grit is about internal drive, not external reward. Signs a player is externally motivated include the following:

- They compete to be recognized and appreciated by others.
- They compete to impress, please, or repay others (coaches, family, etc.).
- They compete for compliments that make them feel better about themselves.
- They worry about what others think of them.
- They compete to feel accepted and a part of the team.

Self-Confidence and Motivation

It is important to couple motivation with belief in your own abilities. Your confidence and self-image determine how much you believe in yourself and in your abilities to become a successful hockey player. Without belief in your ability to be successful, there is little reason to believe that all of your hard work will pay off, which can result in low motivation and a lack of grit.

The link between self-image and motivation is one reason we have taken time in this chapter to formulate a picture of your particular strengths and weaknesses. Your understanding of your skill, commitment, and self-confidence will affect what happens to your game in the coming years. The ultimate goal is to have a realistic view of self, coupled with the self-confidence necessary to work hard and display grit. Consider the following lists and determine whether you display high or low self-confidence:

High Self-Confidence
- You try harder.
- You persist longer.
- You take on greater challenges.
- You are more optimistic.
- You feel less anxious.

Low Self-Confidence
- You are more likely to bail when challenged.
- You don't challenge yourself.
- You feel overwhelmed by difficulty.
- You are negative about yourself and about hockey.

Orientation and Motivation

Orientation is one of those sport-psych concepts that you'll sometimes hear, but it's important to understand what exactly it means because of the influence it can have on your motivation and drive. Simply put, orientation relates to your overall hockey mindset and is defined as the subconscious rules you use to measure your accomplishments as either successful or unsuccessful. A player's orientation is usually one of two styles: ego-oriented or task-oriented.

Ego Orientation

Ego-oriented players constantly compare themselves to the players around them. They judge their success based on how well they're playing compared to their teammates or players on other teams. They measure success by not being the worst player on the team and tend to put more emphasis on winning as opposed to developing their game. They're often heavily externally motivated, with the ego-oriented goals of being better than others, being on the right team, having the right gear, and being a naturally good player.

Task Orientation

Task-oriented players want to master the game and be the best because of how it makes them feel, not because of how they compare to others. Their drive comes from the desire to master certain skills and feel confident in their ability to perform. These players are internally motivated and measure their success by ongoing improvement and how they compare to their performance last week or last season. Their goals are playing with a high compete level, working well with their teammates, and having fun.

Which Is Better?

While it may seem that task orientation is better than ego orientation from a motivational standpoint, they're both very important to developing a competitive mindset. Having the drive and motivation to master skills in hockey builds confidence to work hard and play at your best. However, being driven and motivated to compete and beat your opponent creates the competitive drive and determination to win. They're both important.

Look at guys like Patrick Kane, Sidney Crosby, Connor McDavid, T. J. Oshie, Steven Stamkos, Carey Price, John Tavares, and Drew Doughty. They demonstrate the necessary balance of having both task

and ego orientation. They all work extremely hard to develop their skills; at the same time, when they hit the ice, they want to dominate the players they play against. Understanding this balance helps you improve both your development and will to win. The best players are both task and ego oriented.

To stand out, you should know where you stand in comparison to others. Being ego oriented helps you develop a realistic perspective of where you are skill wise in comparison to others. Once you understand where you stand, it's important to rev up your task orientation, put your head down, and work your butt off to be better today than you were yesterday. Then when you hit the ice against top-ranked opponents, they will know they're up against a fierce and hungry competitor.

Control and Motivation

Another key tenet in maintaining motivation is distinguishing between the things you have control over and the things you can't control. More important, you must understand the amount of focus to devote to each.

Hockey players who focus and work on those things they can control are far more likely to be motivated than players who spend a lot of time focused on—worried about—things over which they have no control.

What Can You Control?

- As a hockey player, there are a number of things you can control:
- How hard you practice
- How hard you play

- Where you place your focus
- How much time you put toward mastering your game
- How you respond to setbacks and adversity
- Your compete level and work ethic

Take a minute and list five things you can control in hockey. Think about your overall hockey development and what you can control in practice, games, and off-ice training.

What Can't You Control?

Now let's look at factors beyond your control:

- The skill or preparation of the other team
- The mood of your coach
- How your teammates are playing
- Crowd noise
- Time and location of your game
- Rink conditions
- What others are thinking

When you think about it, there are a lot of things over which you have absolutely no control. It doesn't mean these concerns don't matter or won't make a difference; it's just that, no matter how you slice it, you really have no control over them. Take a minute and list some factors in your hockey world that are beyond your control.

Focus on the Controllable

Your goal is to understand what you can and can't control in hockey and to go on a mission to maximize your efforts on the controllable while learning how to handle the uncontrollable. If you find yourself agonizing over factors beyond your control, then it is time to change your focus. Worrying about factors beyond your control will not only demotivate you, but it will also steal the mental energy you need to control those things over which you do have influence.

Accountability and Motivation

Character is an important aspect of player development, and when it comes to motivation, the character trait of accountability is common with players who have high levels of motivation. While we don't like to think about failure, we all fail from time to time. The question is, when you do fail, how do you respond? Most players step up and take responsibility for personal and team performance, but sometimes you'll find players who put the blame on someone or something else, essentially handing control of the situation to an outside variable.

I find that players who are accountable for their actions and accept responsibility for individual and team setbacks are far more likely to make an effort to improve and avoid experiencing similar situations in the future. These players are motivated to improve, and that motivation becomes part of their drive. Players who blame outside forces for failure are less motivated and miss out on the learning that can come from facing a setback.

Think back to some of the situations where you have come up short or downright failed. How did you respond? What was your reaction? Were you resolved to get back at it or frustrated and not really interested in getting back in the saddle? Take an honest look at your last setback:

1. What factors led to the setback?
2. What role did you play?
3. What improvements do you need to make, or what areas of your game should you work on to avoid a similar situation?

The Zone and Motivation

Playing "in the zone" in hockey is what every player wants; it's the Holy Grail of hockey. Once players feel it, they're more motivated to find that state again. The term was first coined by tennis players; however, you now hear the term used in just about every sport. Yet, no matter what sport an athlete plays, the descriptions of the phenomenon are remarkably similar. The zone is a magical period of perfection for players in which they seem to find that extra gear. They feel uncharacteristic surges of speed and strength, while at the same time sensing an extraordinary mental serenity or inner stillness, which allows them to play with confidence and trust.

How Can I Find the Zone?

Finding the zone can be rare and elusive, but once you experience it, you'll know it was totally worth the hard work to get there. Getting into the zone is about balancing the right amount of challenge (difficulty) with the right amount of skill (ability). It is as if the speed and pace of the game slows down and your effort and results are positive, easy, and super fun.

Flow and Motivation

"Flow" is another way to describe being in the zone. Flow is finding a rhythm with your activity in which you are totally immersed in your enjoyment of the process. Flow requires focus, so it is important to play at a level that keeps you challenged. On the other hand, too much challenge can cause anxiety and frustration, which can extinguish any sense of flow. Since focus is essential, it's important to find that balance of challenge and ability—if you want to find the zone.

Keys to Motivation

Because motivation is pivotal to grit, you must recognize your level of motivation and consider ways you can increase your inner drive. It may be useful to keep the following precepts in mind:

- Motivation starts with a sense of purpose and continues with intentionally pursuing your goals.

- Learn what motivates you. Is it team performance or individual performance? Focus on those things that motivate you the most.

- Push the edge. Find a weakness in your game and get excited about where your game will be after you fix it. Then develop a plan to fix it.

- Allow yourself to experience success. Set goals for skill mastery and then go step-by-step, starting with mastery of easier skills and progressing to more difficult ones.

- Change your thinking. Use failure to propel you to success. Then forget the failure but remember your successes forever.

- Get involved in your success. Take ownership of your training goals and methods. Work with your coach to establish goals and discuss ways you can achieve those goals.

- Praise others for their successes. If you can't recognize success in others, you won't be able to recognize it in yourself. Finding the positives about the play of others will help you to discover and focus on the positives in your play.

- Vary your training by keeping it challenging enough to be interesting but not so challenging that it makes you frustrated.

- Stay physically healthy so that unmet basic needs don't pull your focus away from your game.
- Surround yourself with motivated people.
- Replace negative thoughts with positive ones.

Take time to remember your personal dreams and goals. Visualize achieving your goals and post them where you can see them often.

Breaking Free of Self-Destructive Thought Patterns

Why is it we can be so kind to others but so hard on ourselves? Actually, from a psychological standpoint, this is a very common occurrence. Research tells us that negative thinking and negative self-talk are mental programming leftover from when we were kids.

Think back to when you were growing up and getting into everything. Maybe you were a wild child or maybe you were careful to follow the rules. Either way, you constantly heard, "Don't do that; stop that; put that down; don't touch that; leave your sister or brother alone." Let's face it, as much as Mom and Dad love us, they're awfully bossy. And I say that with a smile on my face because they do love us and that's why they protect us—even from ourselves. The problem is, all that programming over the years creates a little voice in our heads that picks up where they left off.

When you do something dumb, there's a pretty good chance you'll say to yourself, *Dummy,* or if you messed something up, you'll say, *What's wrong with you?* The internal critic telling us what to do, and doing it in a mean way, is evolution's way of trying to keep us safe and protected. The problem is, it goes too far. Instead of criticizing what we did, it criticizes who we are. Instead of thinking, *That was dumb,* when you put an empty milk container back in the fridge, you think, *I'm dumb for doing it.* Your inner voice has been trained so well to keep you in check that it can go too far.

So, what do you do when you hear that internal critic in your ear, telling you you're an idiot? Just because this may be your current way of thinking doesn't mean you are stuck in the trap forever. For one, it's pretty common. I would bet that nine people out of ten deal with

this internal critic as much or more than you do. But the good thing is, you can break free of these negative thought responses and reprogram your mind to stop being so critical. But it does take awareness, practice, and strategies. Here are some steps you can take to adjust your thinking:

- Realize that how you think about yourself affects how you behave and perform. Did you write this down from earlier? If you didn't, write it down now. THIS IS KEY!
- Visualize yourself as a success. When you catch yourself in a negative thought pattern, immediately replace the thought and visualize success instead. It's very important to learn how to do this!
- Identify your false beliefs about yourself and change them to positive images.
- Set goals that will lead to your success. If you don't know where you're going, how will you know when you get there? Goals are the mark of champions and we will talk about them in the next chapter.
- Focus on those aspects of your personality that will make you a success. Celebrate your strengths and work on your weaknesses—no judgment, just focused effort.

- When you do have a negative experience, learn from it
  and use it as a means of propelling yourself to greater
  heights. Within every adversity is the seed for an equal
  or greater opportunity.

Now that you have more insight into the player you are, we will build on this understanding to clarify your purpose: what it is you want, and what it will take to get it. These are important considerations because, without a plan, you can end up somewhere you never intended to go and waste important opportunities along the way. Now is the time to define your mission. A clear sense of purpose will give you the best shot at achieving all you want out of hockey.

Chapter 4

Purpose

Keith Jones wasn't your prototypical hockey pro. Growing up in the same town as Wayne Gretzky, Keith played in Gretzky's shadow his entire career. He came from a hardworking family and, despite experiencing tragedy at an early age with the loss of his brother, Keith believed he would be a pro hockey player one day. Keith didn't know how, but he knew hockey was his purpose in life.

Coming up through the ranks, "Jonesy," as everyone called him, was on a clearly defined course. As a kid he would write down, on little slips of paper, all the steps it would take to become a pro: AA, AAA, junior, minor pro, and then pro.

When he wasn't drafted to major junior, he was crushed but understood. And because he knew his purpose was to become a professional hockey player one day, he made the necessary adjustments to his plan and kept moving forward. Although not part of his original plan, he ended up getting a full scholarship to play at Western Michigan. Through it all, if there was one distinction to his improbable hockey career, it was his ability to keep showing up, even when better players were quitting all around him.

Drafted by the Washington Capitals, he was cut on the last day of camp. He told the coaches they were making a mistake and promised they would be calling him back within the month. And, while it wasn't exactly a month, he was called up a short while later and was able to stick with the team from that point forward.

Jonesy went on to play 491 games in the NHL and is currently a popular national TV analyst. Although an outsider may consider his an improbable hockey career, Keith Jones knew all along he would be a professional hockey player one day. It was his single-minded purpose that allowed him to check off all the steps on those little slips of paper and arrive at everything he ever wanted.

You see, Jonesy had a plan. He had a goal and went on a mission to achieve it. Even with setbacks and obstacles along the way, his clear sense of purpose kept him moving forward.

While passion is the energy that fuels your drive, your purpose is the inner knowing that can make your dreams a reality. Nothing happens without action. Purpose is setting your intention and creating an action plan to convert passion into reality.

Here's what you need to know about the top performers in all areas of society, not just hockey: they all made conscious decisions to become their best and realize their purpose. The following statements describe the trajectory of the greatest achievers:

- They have a clear vision of what they want to achieve and know the path to take.
- They set goals and review them often.

- They view their goals as having extreme importance in
  their life.
- They are willing to do whatever it takes to achieve their
  goals, working longer and harder than others.

When most players think about their purpose and path, they immediately want to work on goal setting. However, it is only when your self-image, values, and goals are aligned that you're truly happy with where you're going and ready to take action. So let's set this process in motion by discussing self-image.

Self-Image

As we discussed in the last chapter, self-perception is crucial. Understanding your personality type, your strengths, and your weaknesses is an important component in developing grit. Let's now consider how self-perception shapes your self-image and how self-image shapes your goals. After working with hundreds of players over the years, I can tell you, what you believe about yourself molds your sense of purpose and is a predictor of what you will achieve. What you believe about yourself informs your self-image:

- Your self-image defines the expectations you have for
  yourself, and it influences the goals you set.
- A strong and positive self-image puts you on the path
  to achieving your full potential.
- A positive self-image opens the possibilities of the
  world for you and allows you to work toward anything
  you want.
- A limited or negative self-image holds you back and
  limits your potential, much like driving a high-powered
  sports car with the parking brake on.

In short, your self-image is how you see yourself in your mental mirror. It's who you think you are, what you think you can do, and where you think you can go.

Your Mental Blueprint

You have a mental blueprint inside of you, a collection of thoughts and beliefs about yourself. It is made of your past experiences, your perception of how others view you, and how you view yourself. Whether this blueprint is accurate hardly matters because what you believe to be true about yourself will influence how you think, feel, and, ultimately, perform.

When you believe something to be true about yourself, you will act in a manner that continues to support that mental blueprint. If your self-image is positive, you will have the confidence to go after the things you want. If your self-image is poor, you may get caught in a negative loop and never realize your potential.

Though nobody sets out to have a poor self-image, it happens. Human beings tend to focus on the negative, giving greater weight to the bad while downplaying the good. They also tend to emphasize recent events over past history. If you've played strong hockey for several seasons but then have a stretch of bad games, you naturally fear you're falling into a slump when, in fact, you've just had a few bad games amidst many good ones.

When you identify with failure and disappointment, you are sending your psyche a powerful message: *Don't expect much; set the bar low.* Thoughts like these do not make the elite player. Ask yourself the following questions and consider whether your mental blueprint is positive or negative:

1. Do I focus more on my failures than on my successes?
2. When I experience disappointment, can I get past it, or do I dwell on it?
3. When something goes wrong, do I typically blame myself?
4. Do I replay my mistakes over and over in my head?
5. Do I personalize losses and disappointments? (For instance, if something doesn't work out, I think, *Boy, I really stink. How can I be such an idiot?!*)
6. Can I give myself a break, or am I my harshest critic?

If you identify with these questions, you may be crafting a negative self-image, setting yourself up for low self-confidence and low achievement.

We all act in a way that is consistent with our self-image, whether that self-image is accurate or not. For instance, if you believe you can't perform under pressure, then every time you feel pressure, your mental blueprint tells you to give up. It's important to remember that when you think of yourself in a certain way, you will eventually create that reality.

The Importance of Confidence

Confidence in hockey is a huge factor, often separating the good players from the great. Most coaches will tell you it is the most important mental skill a player can possess. When you play with confidence, you trust your skills and ability; your game is natural and free. To consistently play at the upper end of your ability, you must play with confidence. It is the foundation of your mental game, and, without it, you will struggle to reach your true potential.

Confidence is the strength of your belief that you can execute the right skill at the right time at a high level. Whether it's skating, stickhandling, or puck stopping, how confident you are in your abilities will determine your execution. Your true hockey performance will be a direct reflection of your high level of confidence, which comes from working hard and being successful in practice and then carrying this assurance to your game.

You build confidence in both games and practice. In practice, there is less pressure and more time to pay attention to executing skills correctly, all of which builds a positive, self-assured feeling. Game confidence comes from knowing that the skills you've worked on in practice, and throughout the season, will be there when you need them.

As your confidence grows, you'll begin to feel more comfortable and relaxed. You will gain a greater sense of purpose and believe achieving your goals is possible. As you relax and begin to trust your game, your level of play will also increase. This begins a cycle of positive reinforcement, where increased confidence leads to better performance, which, in turn, leads to even more confidence. Your growing confidence also becomes a shield, protecting you from the negative comments and judgments of others.

The more you develop your hockey skills, the better you will play and the less likely you will be to take to heart the negative comments of others. Through practice, training, and game experience, you will be better able to assess your own abilities, and your assessment will take priority over the appraisal of others.

Developing and maintaining this rock-solid assurance doesn't always come naturally, but there are things you can do to build and strengthen your confidence and self-image. Most of you have access to a note-taking app. If not, download one and begin to pay attention to what you think about. In chapter 3 we talked about self-awareness, but for this exercise, I just want you to use your smartphone to keep notes about what you think about.

You may be thinking to yourself, *Aw, man, I don't need to keep notes; I'll remember.* My answer is, no, you won't. You will forget. I am 100 percent sure you will forget. So, please just do me a favor and keep notes about what you're thinking. Every time you catch yourself thinking a negative thought or ruminating on beliefs that hurt your self-image, immediately pull out your smartphone and jot down the negative thought. Next, take a minute to reframe that thought and rewrite it as a positive one.

This might feel weird at first. Reframing your thoughts might seem like you are lying to yourself. However, it is important to understand that every thought you have is programming your brain. When you have the negative thought, you are programming and reinforcing a negative mindset. But when you come right back with a positive thought, you disrupt the negative programming and create positive programming, supported by the positive thought.

Challenging negative beliefs doesn't happen overnight. It can feel strange, but the more you challenge negative beliefs with positive beliefs, the more your brain will change to support the new belief. So, remember, if you feel trapped by low confidence or a poor self-image, it doesn't have to be that way. Building confidence and a strong self-image is all in the way you think. To be who you want to be and fulfill your purpose in hockey, just describe yourself the way you want to be seen. Essentially, you have a choice in your self-talk; you just need to choose who you want to be.

That's right. A large part of your future is up to you; you have a choice. I know it sounds simple, but this is how success is achieved. It starts in your mind as you choose the kind of athlete you want to be. If you're not who you want to be right now, then choose other thoughts, another vision.

If you are stuck with negative beliefs about yourself, you're not alone. This is a common issue faced not only by athletes, but also by people in all walks of life. We get stuck in belief systems we assume are true, so we never question them. We then believe we're a certain way, even if the evidence does not support the image. The way to beat this is to actively choose who you want to be.

How can you do that? Get out your smartphone and jot down ten positive statements, using the adjectives you want to be true descriptors of you.

Here's a good example. I worked with a junior defenseman who was a very good player. He was playing junior A in Calgary and getting time with his major junior club as well. His coach and teammates loved him. The problem was, although he had elite skill, he struggled with his compete level. He was a quiet guy and that subdued personality followed him onto the ice.

Doing this word choice exercise with him, I noticed he didn't choose the words *intense* or *competitive*. I asked him why, and he said he just didn't see himself that way. I asked about his favorite player, and he told me it was Drew Doughty. I asked if he thought Drew Doughty was a fierce, intense competitor. He said, "Absolutely, without question."

So, I asked him to think of words that describe Drew Doughty and then turn them into positive statements about himself. Here are a few:

- "I am a very intense player on the ice, and I use that intensity to psych out my opponent."
- "I am a fierce competitor; I outwork and out battle everyone."
- "My focus and intensity at the start of the game allow me to get off to a fast start."

I had him write down ten statements, describing himself the way he wanted to be rather than the way he thought he was now. Learning how to act *as if* will help in this area. More on this topic later in the book.

Now you do the same thing. Write ten empowering statements you can review each week. Declaring what you want to see is how you become the player you want to be. You will actually change the programming in your brain.

As you do this exercise, keep in mind the following list of confidence and positive self-image saboteurs:

- **Thoughts about yourself will affect your confidence and self-image.** For example, if you think, *I am not very smart*, you are sending a powerful negative message to yourself, and it's highly likely you will prove yourself right. If your goal is to be stupid, keep telling yourself you're not smart.

- **Beliefs about your skills, abilities, worth, and value will affect your confidence and self-image.** If you believe you have the skills to get the job done on the ice, that's called confidence. On the other hand, if you avoid being on the ice when the game is on the line or worry you will be the player who makes the mistake to lose the game, then your confidence and self-image may be hurting your development. Maybe you've heard the saying, "If you think you can or you think you can't, you're right!" Remember, you become what you think about, so pay attention to what you think.

- **Feelings you have about yourself will affect your confidence and self-image.** If you are constantly frustrated or down on yourself, it is likely your confidence will suffer. Frustration, anxiety, anger, and doubt are severe energy drains and will leave you mentally and physically weak.

- **Your internal critic will affect your confidence and self-image.** That nagging little voice in your head that critiques your every move on the ice can kill your confidence. Let me ask you a question: how do you feel when someone calls you an idiot? Well, it's no different when you call yourself an idiot over and over and over again in your mind—yet many players do this all the time. This damaging self-talk needs to stop.

- **The situations in which you put yourself will affect your confidence and self-image.** If you put yourself in situations beyond your skill level, your confidence will probably take a hit. If, on the other hand, you put yourself in situations where you're forced to work hard and the hard work brings success, that's a great situation for developing your confidence and a strong, positive self-image.

How would you rate your confidence and self-image? Players with strong confidence and a healthy self-image do the following:

- They accurately assess themselves and their ability. They have a good grasp on their strengths and weaknesses and put themselves in situations where, *if they work hard*, they can excel.

- They accept who they are, *without judgment*. They don't beat themselves up or become their own worst enemy. They don't minimize their accomplishments; rather, they give themselves credit for how far they've come.

In contrast, players with low confidence and a poor self-image do the following:

- They rely on how they are doing in the present moment to determine how they feel about themselves. If they're playing well, they like themselves; if they're playing poorly, then they hate themselves.

- They need positive, *external* experiences to counteract the negative feelings and thoughts that constantly plague them. They rely on positive feedback from others to build up their self-image. When they get down, they need others to build them up because they have a hard time building themselves back up.
- They think feeling good is only temporary and believe it's just a matter of time before they're down again.

Reprogramming Your Self-Image for Success

We have established there are many thoughts and beliefs that go on beneath the surface, subconsciously, influencing your confidence—positively or negatively. Self-talk is programming your self-image, whether you think it is or not. When you're on the ice and make a mistake, do you criticize yourself and beat yourself up? If so, you're programming your brain to believe you are a loser. Is that the programming you want in your brain? This must stop! Your job is to interrupt this negative cycle and reprogram your competitive mind the right way.

How can you break free of the downward spiral? By consciously interrupting the negative thoughts. Again, the answer starts with awareness. As soon as you catch yourself making a negative value judgment, do the following:

- **Cancel the negative judgment.** As soon as you catch yourself thinking negatively, stop. You can literally say "stop" or "no," out loud if you want, to disrupt the thought.
- **Replace the negative value judgment with a positive one.** For instance, if you find yourself thinking, *I always choke under pressure*, change it to, *I step up in big games; my defensive play gives us a chance to win.*

- **Affirm your new statement.** As soon as you can, write down your new statement and say it daily. Compile a list of all new statements.
- **Act as if.** In other words, fake it. If your new statement is, *I am confident in games,* but you really don't feel confident, act confident anyway. Sit up and get a little cocky. Adopt a confident posture, facial expression, and tone. Believe it or not, if you act confident, you'll soon start to feel confident, and sometimes that's just what you need to break out of a negative way of thinking.

Now that we understand how positive self-image and confidence contribute to a sense of purpose, we are ready to consider the role values play in setting goals.

Values

To define your purpose in hockey, you must understand your personal values and identify what's truly important in your life—not just your hockey life, but in your life overall. Once you identify your values and understand they are your motivating force, you can put together your mission for achieving your goals.

Have you ever taken on a goal that sounded good and was supported by others, but, for some reason, just didn't sit right? You knew it was a worthy goal, but it felt a little off. It might have felt false because it didn't align with your values.

For example, when I turned sixteen, I bought a motocross motorcycle from a friend. It wasn't new, but it ran great, and I had a ton of fun with it. I took that bike everywhere. There was a place not far from my house called the Pits, with hills and jumps and everything a good motocross track should have.

A year later, I was ready to upgrade, and that meant I needed to sell the bike. Did I mention I rode that bike hard? The bike wasn't perfect by this point, but it was still a good bike. So, I set a goal to sell it so I could raise money toward a new bike. I decided to ask for one thousand dollars. The bike ran great, but the gears would stick occasionally—nothing big and nothing a little elbow grease couldn't fix.

So, I placed an ad; within days, I had several good offers. I wasn't really telling anyone about the gears and was sticking to my thousand-dollar asking price. But I felt weird. One guy offered me $975, and I said no. Another guy offered one thousand but needed to make payments. I said no again.

My dad asked me why I kept saying no, and, to be honest, I wasn't sure. I knew I wanted to sell the bike but why was I hesitating? Then my dad put on his Dr. Phil hat and asked me how the bike ran, and I told him about the sticky gears. Then he asked if I had mentioned this to  any of the potential buyers, and I had to be honest and tell him I didn't.

Giving me that look dads can give you, he suggested that I tell the next person about the gears and see what happens. So, the next day, I had a guy who really wanted it but only had nine hundred dollars. I told him about the gears, and he said he didn't care. He really liked the bike. After telling him about the sticky gears, I felt so much better, and I really wanted him to have it, even if his offer was lower than what I was asking.

Back then, a hundred dollars was a lot of money to me, so taking less but feeling better didn't seem logical. But I took the money and felt really good about the whole transaction. It wasn't until years later, going through my own course on values in college, that I remembered selling that bike. Learning about values and being true to yourself, I was able to make sense of the situation.

I struggled selling the bike for more money because I wasn't being honest with the people looking to buy it. I wasn't being dishonest, but I wasn't being up-front either. I have since realized honesty and authenticity are two of my top values. Trying to sell the bike without telling buyers about the gears wasn't honest. I didn't consciously realize it at the time, but I wasn't able to let myself sell it until I shared everything about the bike.

This was a powerful lesson for me. It was real-life proof that my values must align with my goals and actions; otherwise, I was not being true to myself. And, it's still a good example of how who we are needs to align with what we want out of life.

So, this is why, before setting your goals, you must understand your personal values and clarify what is essential: What is important to you? What do you want your life to stand for? What sort of qualities do you want to develop and express as a person?

Values are our heart's deepest desires for the way we want to interact with and relate to other people, and ourselves. They are leading principles that can guide us and motivate us as we move through life. Values reflect what we want to do and how we want to do it. They influence how you want to behave with your friends, your family, your team, and your environment.

Values are not the same as goals. Values involve ongoing action; they are like directions we move in, whereas goals are what we want to achieve along the way. Goals can be achieved or "crossed off," whereas values are part of you. Values are ongoing and serve as a sort of compass, keeping you on the path to what's most important in life. So, while values and goals are related, we now understand the distinction and the reason it is important to consider personal values before setting goals.

Common Values

Now, let's make these concepts personally relevant. Let's determine what you value most in life. Once you are clear on your values, you can be sure to set goals that will sync up with what is most important to you.

Look at the following list of fifty-seven common values. I've compiled this list after years of working with players, coaches, and parents. However, if there is a value you consider important and don't see it on the list, then by all means add it.

Your job is to go through the list and put either a "V" for very important, an "S" for somewhat important, or an "N" for not important. When you are finished, each value will be marked with a letter.

- **Acceptance:** to be open to and accepting of myself, others, life, and so on
- **Adventure:** to be adventurous; to actively seek, create, or explore novel or stimulating experiences
- **Assertiveness:** to respectfully stand up for my rights and request what I want
- **Authenticity:** to be genuine and real; to be true to myself
- **Beauty:** to appreciate, create, nurture, or cultivate beauty in myself, others, the environment, and so on
- **Caring:** to be caring toward myself, others, the environment, and so on
- **Challenge:** to keep challenging myself to grow, learn, and improve
- **Compassion:** to act with kindness toward those who are suffering
- **Conformity:** to be respectful of and obedient to rules and obligations
- **Connection:** to engage fully in whatever I am doing and be fully present with others

- **Contribution:** to help or make a positive difference to myself or others
- **Cooperation:** to cooperate and collaborate with others
- **Courage:** to be brave; to persist in the face of fear, threat, or difficulty
- **Creativity:** to be creative or innovative
- **Curiosity:** to be open-minded and interested; to explore and discover
- **Encouragement:** to reward behavior that I value in myself or others
- **Equality:** to treat others as equal to myself and vice versa
- **Excitement:** to seek, create, and engage in activities that are exciting, stimulating, or thrilling
- **Fairness:** to be fair to myself and others
- **Fitness:** to maintain or improve my fitness; to look after my physical and mental health and well-being
- **Flexibility:** to adjust and adapt readily to changing circumstances
- **Forgiveness:** to be forgiving toward myself and others
- Freedom: to live freely; to choose how I live and behave and to help others do likewise
- **Friendliness:** to be friendly, companionable, or agreeable toward others
- **Fun:** to seek, create, and engage in fun-filled activities
- **Generosity:** to share and be giving, both to myself and others
- **Gratitude:** to be grateful for and appreciative of the positive aspects I see in myself, others, and life in general

- **Honesty:** to be honest, truthful, and sincere with myself and others
- **Humility:** to be humble or modest; to let my achievements speak for themselves
- **Humor:** to see and appreciate the humorous side of life
- Independence: to support myself and choose my own way of doing things
- **Industry:** to be industrious, hardworking, and dedicated
- **Intimacy:** to open up, reveal, and share myself—emotionally or physically—in my close personal relationships
- **Justice:** to uphold justice and fairness
- **Kindness:** to be kind, compassionate, considerate, nurturing, or caring toward myself or others
- **Love:** to act lovingly or affectionately toward myself or others
- **Mindfulness:** to be conscious of, open to, and curious about my here-and-now experience
- **Open-mindedness:** to think things through, see things from others' points of view, and weigh evidence fairly
- **Order:** to be orderly and organized
- **Patience:** to wait calmly and tolerantly for what I want
- **Persistence:** to continue resolutely, despite problems or difficulties
- **Pleasure:** to create and give pleasure to myself or others
- **Power:** to strongly influence or wield authority over others; to take charge, lead, and organize
- **Reciprocity:** to build relationships in which there is a fair balance of giving and taking

- **Respect:** to be respectful toward myself and others; to be polite and considerate, always showing positive regard
- **Responsibility:** to be responsible and accountable for my actions
- **Romance:** to be romantic; to display and express love or strong affection
- **Safety:** to secure, protect, or ensure the safety of myself or others
- **Self-awareness:** to be aware of my own thoughts, feelings, and actions
- **Self-care:** to look after my health and well-being and to get my needs met
- **Self-development:** to keep growing, advancing, or improving in knowledge, skills, character, or life experience
- **Self-control:** to act in accordance with my own ideals
- **Sensuality:** to create, explore, and enjoy experiences that stimulate the five senses
- **Spirituality:** to connect with things bigger than myself
- **Skillfulness:** to continually practice and improve my skills and apply myself fully when using them
- **Supportiveness:** to be supportive, helpful, encouraging, and available to myself or others
- **Trust:** to be trustworthy; to be loyal, faithful, sincere, and reliable

Look only at the values marked "V" and choose the five or six that resonate with you the most. These are your top values. List them below.

My Top Values

1. _____

2. _____

3. _____

4. _____

5. _____

6. _____

Now that you have committed your values to writing, put the list somewhere safe and review it now and again to remind yourself of what's truly important.

As we talk about goal setting in the next section, you can compare possible goals with your values to make sure they are compatible. When your goals and values are in sync, you're not only more likely to achieve your goals, but the pursuit of your goals will also be more enjoyable and fulfilling.

Goals

Goal setting clarifies the purpose behind your effort on the ice. Thoughts, feelings, and emotions will rise and fall like the tides, but your goals are the foundation that keeps you on the path to becoming a Complete Player. Your goals change the uncertainty of "maybe" and "I hope" into "I *can*" and "I *will*."

Clear goals add intensity to your game and provide the focus it takes to practice and play with purpose, rather than winging it or wondering what you should work on. When things are tough or you're down and out, goals pick you up and pull you through.

Types of Goals

Outcome Goals

Outcome goals are—not surprisingly—related to outcomes, the results you want to achieve in a certain time frame. They can be broad in scope: having a winning season or getting into the playoffs. Or, they can be more specific: leading your team in scoring, leading the league in goal-against average, or making the all-star team. Outcome goals can also be divided into long-term (playing hockey in college) or short-term (winning the championship this season). Or, they can be minigoals, like winning the next game or scoring a hat trick.]

The thing about outcome goals is, they require something outside of you; they are not entirely within your control. For example, to have a winning season, you must have a skilled and willing team that is capable of winning. The coach must put together a solid game plan to beat the other teams in your league, and you and your teammates must be dedicated and focused in practice.

If you want to lead the league in scoring, you must have line mates who move the puck. You need a regular shift throughout the season. Goalies who want the lowest goals against average (GAA) need defensemen who play smart, defensive hockey. They need forwards who come back and help the defense. You see, not all these factors are within one player's control.

Because outcome goals include factors beyond your control, you want to make sure you are not choosing outcome goals exclusively. Let's talk about the other types of goals you want to include.

Performance Goals

Performance goals are goals in which you challenge yourself. It's you against you. In contrast to outcome goals, performance goals aren't dependent on what anyone else in the league does. For example, you can improve your speed, add ten pounds of muscle in the off-season, win more puck battles, and get more shots on net if you set your mind to it.

With performance goals, you ask yourself, What did I do last season? How can I do better? What do I need to work on to improve my grit? You pinpoint how to improve, and you get to work.

As you set performance goals, remember you must have a way to measure your progress. You can't have a goal to win more puck battles if you don't know how many you won last game or last season. When you pick performance goals, determine how to track and measure your development. When chosen wisely and measured consistently, performance goals can be powerful motivators.

Players, coaches, and parents often ask me if they should share their performance goals with others. Here's what I tell them: sharing your goals is a personal decision. If you trust those you are sharing with and feel they can help you along the way, then, by all means, share. If, on the other hand, it just doesn't feel right to tell others your personal goals, then keep them private.

I personally find that motivation increases in those who openly share their goals. When you tell others about a goal, you then care what they think of your progress. You want them to see you as a winner, an achiever. As humans, we tend to work harder for the approval of others than we do for ourselves. For that reason, sharing a goal may be more effective than making a quiet declaration in your mind.

Finding good performance goals is easy. Here are just a few: shutting down the other team's best player, doing three sets of ten reps

on the bench press, hitting five stations in your next workout, or getting your workout done in forty-five minutes. These are all worthwhile goals. You just need to pick the ones that move you in the direction you want to go.

Just because you can pick one hundred different goals doesn't mean you should. Too many goals can be just as bad as having no goals at all. Goals are not about quantity; they're about quality. So, don't pick one hundred; rather, pick three to five that clearly relate to your values and will take you where you want to go.

Process Goals

Process goals relate to the very specific skills you execute in practice and games: you skate, you pass, you hustle, you battle, you stickhandle, you stop pucks, you forecheck, you backcheck, and on and on. These are skills particular to hockey, and they are also process goals.

When working with players, I call these goals "your ABCs," something I learned from Dr. Miller's book *Hockey Tough*. Your ABCs are things you do every game, specific skills that, when executed properly, help you have a great game.[5]

Your ABCs, for the most part, are automatic habits, things you do without thinking. But by deliberately setting your ABCs (process goals), you can improve your mental game and willfully improve the skills you've put on autopilot. When you get distracted or upset, you can use your ABCs to restore focus and get your head back in the game. You can take those small, mechanical skills and make them better by focusing on and honing them in practice. And this is where good coaching comes in. Good coaches help you learn subtle but powerful tweaks to your game that give you a leg up on others.

So, let's review. An outcome goal would be to make the all-star team. A performance goal would be to get faster and more agile on your skates. And process goals would include keeping your feet moving, bending your knees, and keeping your weight on your inside edge on tight turns. Can you see how these different types of goals all come together to improve your game?

SMART Goals

For each of your outcome, performance, and process goals, you'll want to set SMART goals. SMART stands for specific, measurable, attainable, relevant, and time-based. Let's consider each of these factors.

Specific

Rather than setting a goal to play "good," establish a more specific goal to win 50 percent of your faceoffs. Don't be general with your description. Having a goal to "have a good game" could mean anything. Instead, choose goals that explicitly describe what it means to have a good game or a good season. For instance, aiming to make five to ten shots on net or neutralize the other team's top line are distinct process goals for a game. You can't control every outcome, and you can't control others, but if your goal is to have a good game, make sure you define what that means.

Measurable

Anything you can measure can be turned into a goal, but a goal you cannot measure simply does not work. Otherwise, how will you know you are successful? Pick goals you can measure, monitor, and track. You can count shots on goals or puck battles won. You can track the number of goals scored against you and the number of minutes you played. Those are performance goals you can easily evaluate.

Attainable

The next key to formulating a SMART goal is to choose something attainable. When we say a goal should be attainable, we don't mean easy—but we don't mean impossible either. A SMART goal is something you can reach if you work hard; it's something that stretches you but doesn't break you. Big, bold goals are awesome, especially when framed in a way that you sense you can achieve it, but only if you give it dedicated, committed, focused effort. That balance of audacity and realism is exactly what you want in a goal. Making the all-star team is an attainable outcome goal if you are willing to work hard and remain focused during the season.

Relevant and Realistic

Relevant goals support each other, feed into each other, and clearly relate to the ultimate outcome you hope to achieve. Having a goal to sing lead in the school play is a good goal, but it's not a goal that will help you on your path to playing elite hockey. Realistic goals are attainable; you won't be defeated by overshooting what's reasonable to expect at your particular stage. If it's too bold, too unrealistic, such that all the planets must align just right, then the goal can make you feel defeated—the opposite of what we are trying to accomplish.

So, make sure your goal is possible by being honest with yourself about your skills and potential. If you think you can be drafted to the NHL out of peewee, that's an unrealistic goal. However, if you think you can be the next Connor McDavid, that's not completely unrealistic, but it's most likely a huge leap from where you are now.

To reach your McDavid goal, you will need to achieve other big goals along the way: to play major junior or college, to be the top scorer on your team, or to be the top scorer in the league. These are all realistic and would be reasonable goals if you hope to make the McDavid goal happen. But remember, too, being the top scorer in the league requires a lot of things to fall into place, so be honest and realistic about where you are and what you need to do to stay on that path.

Sometimes, when I talk about realistic and unrealistic goals, I wonder if I'm bumming players out. I don't ever want you to doubt your abilities, but I also do not want you to set only easy goals. Easy goals won't make you a better player. They might make you feel good for a little while, but they won't make you a better player.

My hope for you is that you will learn to set goals that inspire you to follow your dream. Pick big goals, pick bold goals, but just make sure there is a real path to reaching them. When you refine your goals so they feel real and possible, it will inspire your motivation and drive.

Time-Based

The last element of a SMART goal is that it must be time-based. It cannot be an open-ended wish with no timetable or deadline. For your goals to be effective, they need to have some sort of timeline, perhaps a season or a game. It could also be a long-term goal, like playing hockey in college, but a bold goal with no end point means nothing. To make it real, you must set an expiration date. For example, you could challenge yourself to become the top defenseman on your team this season. That's an excellent performance goal, and because you framed it in the season, it's specific, measurable, attainable, realistic, and time-based.

Taking Action

Having goals is important but actually working toward them is the real purpose of goal setting. Be careful that you don't see setting goals and planning your mission as the goal itself. You won't achieve anything if you get stuck in the planning and dreaming stage. I know this seems super obvious, but I've seen many players stall.

Have you ever bought a book on an interesting topic you wanted to learn all about? Did you read past the first chapter? Be honest. Everybody gets excited about a new plan, a new venture, but it's the execution of the plan that counts.

The reason we fail to put in the work is because, by buying the book, we feel we've already accomplished something. We had the thought, and now we have a book to support the thought. The information we plan to learn is right at our fingertips anytime we want it. It seems just owning the book will make us smarter on the topic.

But that's not how it works. We must read the book for the book to be useful. Similarly, writing down goals may feel like we've done something final and resolute, but goal setting is just the beginning. Now it's time to do the work. So how do we make sure we're taking purposeful action?

Well, it's simple. Make sure all your goals have actionable items you can work on every day to move you closer to the big goal. Always ask yourself: what can I do today that will move me closer to one or more of my goals? If your goal is to be the top scorer on your team, what can you do today to help with that? You could shoot pucks, right? You could get in the driveway and fire one hundred pucks at the garage door (sorry, Mom and Dad).

At practice, work on your skating, your moves, your hands, and your snipes. Practice where you release the puck when shooting; practice using players as screens; practice your moves in tight areas. Break down every goal into specific tasks and then work on each of them.

How about when it's game time? What specific tasks will help you meet your goal? I'm not telling you to be selfish or a puck hog, but if you want to be a top scorer in the league, you better get shots on net and create scoring chances. If you're not successful and feel off track with achieving your goal, you better know why and have a plan to work on it.

Another way to take action toward your goal is watch a lot of hockey. Watch Crosby, McDavid, Kane, Matthews, and Ovechkin. These guys score a lot. How do they do it? Model your game after what they do.

Growing up, Connor McDavid had a daily goal to run drills. He would come home from school and set up an obstacle course in his driveway—not just some days, but every day! He didn't miss a single day, and he fought to run these drills better and faster than the day before. He would drill and drill and drill and work on these skills until he could do them at top speed without messing up.

Can you honestly say you have a clear goal like that? Do you have goals with specific and measurable tasks that you can work to accomplish every day? And do you have the dedication, persistence, and commitment to do what's necessary to move along the path toward your goals? If not, why?

The bottom line is this: without goals, it will be difficult—maybe even impossible—to achieve all the things you want. Goals provide the roadmap for your hockey achievement, so choose wisely and work unwaveringly.

Now you can add these goal-setting strategies to the passion, perception, and purpose strategies we have already discussed. As you combine these elements of grit, your game will improve and you will feel inspired to stay the course. Next up, we'll learn how to put your passion and purpose to work by maximizing your efforts in practice. This is called *deliberate practice*, and it is all about going from "just practicing" to practicing with a purpose.

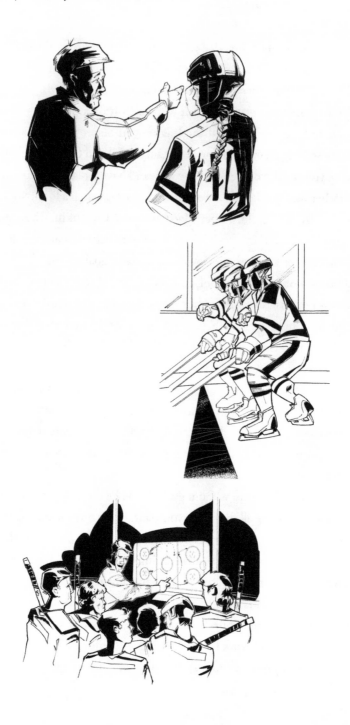

Chapter 5

Practice

Mastery in anything involves continuous study, effort, practice, learning, struggle, and persistence, which takes a lot of time and patience on your part. To consistently improve yourself through deliberate practice, you need to have a solid understanding of self, of where you are now, coupled with the passion, purpose, and perseverance to move forward. Mastery and progress are enhanced when you find a great coach, mentor, or role model who will encourage and guide you as you develop.

Nick wasn't a big guy and always had to outwork his teammates to stay on the top line as he came up the ranks in hockey. Playing in Michigan, where there are a ton of great players all wanting the same thing, Nick learned early on how to work hard in practice. But because he was playing on an elite development team, where everyone works hard and has mad skills, hard work just wasn't enough anymore.

Since Nick didn't have the size, he needed to be smarter than the guy next to him. He needed to be faster, and his skills needed to be sharper if he was to stand out. Fortunately, one of Nick's coaches was a similar-type player. Like Nick, Coach Matt wasn't the biggest guy on the ice, but he had a huge compete level and a ton of skill. Coach Matt taught Nick that if he wanted to stand out on a team full of great players, he needed to practice smarter. He needed to come to practice every day and work on very specific skills until he could execute them automatically at a high level. Coach Matt told Nick, in no uncertain terms, that if he wanted to learn how to play, he needed to learn how to practice.

Practice is where winners are made. Today, Nick is a top line forward playing NCAA D-1 hockey in the Big Ten and is captain of his team. He is preparing to play pro hockey after graduating.

Deliberate practice is the critical tool for unlocking your true potential as a player. Practice can create measurable changes in your mind and body that will generate a lifetime of enhanced performance. Achieving your potential is not a given, and it's certainly not a passive process. Rather, it's an active process that requires you to take intentional, purposeful action. In this chapter, we will learn the difference between practice and deliberate practice and consider factors that ultimately determine how useful your practice time—and recovery time—will be.

The Science of Skill

The key to deliberate practice is working at a level that challenges your abilities, rather than repetitively practicing at a skill level you've already mastered.

Researchers have uncovered something rather remarkable about skill development. Science has demonstrated that developing talent through focused and deliberate practice creates measurable physiological (physical) and psychological (mental) changes in your body, and these changes are what separate the average player from the elite player.

In his book *The Talent Code,* Dan Coyle explains the brain is made up of grey matter (neurons) and white matter (insulating material), and scientists now know how the process called myelination plays a big role in the development of talent.[6] Simply stated, every time you execute a skill or process a thought, brain signals are transmitted throughout your brain along pathways called axons. And the faster and more precise these signals are, the greater your ability to execute that skill repeatedly.

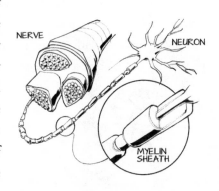

Using these connections in the brain over and over by performing a skill over and over strengthens these connections and wraps layer after layer of insulation, called myelin, around the connections, making them stronger, faster, and more automatic. If you've ever heard someone say, "It's how your brain is wired," this process is what they are talking about. Essentially, you can rewire your brain through deliberate practice, so it's crucial to understand what deliberate practice requires.

Choosing Deliberate Practice

Take a moment to assess yourself and your team. Are you practicing deliberately? Are you intentionally using practice time to work toward your specific goals? If not, how can you start practicing deliberately, beginning today? Remember, world-class performance requires deliberate practice.

Professional players understand deliberate practice, players like Crosby, Ovechkin, Parise, Toews, Kane, Miller, Stamkos, Doughty,

Kopitar, and Keith. How do you think these guys made it to the show? Look at some of the young guns, like McDavid, Matthews, Laine, Werenski, Gaudreau, Kucherov, Ekblad, Eichel, and Pastrnack. Watch them practice; it's incredible. It's no wonder these guys are so good. Pro players practice with speed, intensity, and purpose. They practice *deliberately*, and it's one of the reasons they're playing in the NHL.

Deliberate practice is critical to your growth and improvement, both in hockey and in other areas of your life. While most players I meet tell me they want to be the best, few will do what is necessary to grow their talent to a world-class level. If we know the part practice plays in developing effective, highly skilled, elite players, why do so few players do it with purpose and passion? I list the main reasons below:

- It's hard, hard work!
- It takes focus, perseverance, commitment, and patience.
- It can be a long, difficult, painful process, and not much fun at times.
- Players think others are naturally talented and no amount of practice can make up the difference. (So, why bother?)
- Players don't want success badly enough, or they are unwilling to do what it takes to achieve it.
- Oh, and did I mention, it's hard, hard work?

Only a tiny percentage of hockey players ever make it to the NHL. Why is this? Are they lucky? Were they born destined to play hockey? By now you might know where I'm going with these questions.

The reason so few players ever make it to the NHL is because only a small percentage have the grit and determination to consistently and continuously develop their mind and body through deliberate practice.

How You Practice Matters

Any player who practices the same skill over and over will eventually become proficient. However, if you only practice one aspect of your game, you are not being deliberate and purposeful in your effort. In short, your overall game will not develop. This observation seems obvious, but you would be surprised how many excellent players fall into the trap of choosing easy over intentional.

Compare the player who practices the same old skills to the player who not only works on what he's good at and what comes easily, but also pushes himself, with intention, in skill areas where he's weak or struggling. Again, choosing deliberate, focused practice seems obvious, but I'm telling you, the natural tendency is to work on what we're good at (because it feels instantly satisfying) and avoid areas where we are weak (because it feels intensely frustrating). We do this while telling ourselves, and others, that we are striving to be an elite player.

Because practice is such a critical component to developing grit, let's talk about five essential factors you must incorporate to make sure you are getting the most out of your practice time: master coaching, drills, zone time, repetition, and game-like conditions.

Master Coaching

Deliberate practice requires specific feedback from a reliable, experienced, master coach. True improvement starts by working with a skilled coach who can evaluate weaknesses in an honest and objective fashion. Feedback is critical for improvement, and we cannot do this for ourselves. Insightful, unbiased critique comes only through master coaching.

A master coach possesses a deep knowledge and passion for the game. Because of his expertise, he can provide highly detailed feedback and make targeted adjustments to a player's skill and performance. These coaches have insight into how their players learn best and can target a particular player's personality and method of learning. With this high-quality instruction, players can focus on the specific skills they need to improve to advance their game.

Through a combination of motivation and intensity, master coaches ensure their players don't coast or waste opportunities to learn. The best master coaches are respected, admired, and even feared at times. They are dedicated to making you the best you can be and will push you, even to the point of physical and psychological pain, to help you become your best.

Drills

Deliberate practice consists of specific drills and activities designed to improve performance. Master coaches can diagnose specific issues and tailor drills and activities to help you address them. For instance, a goalie with a weak glove hand may be setting up with his glove in the wrong position. A coach who diagnoses the problem might show him video of his positioning and then work on a series of drills designed to improve his ready position.

By seeing the problem, the goalie can visualize what he needs to improve. By working the glove hand over and over, deliberately challenging himself to make a save and then get back in position, the goalie will rewire his brain and muscles with the correct skill. Shooting more pucks at him day after day isn't going to help him improve if the fundamental position of the glove isn't addressed. Practicing *deliberate, specific* drills over and over is the only way you can make lasting improvement to your game.

Zone Time

To be effective in your practice habits and see results, you must stay in your optimal practice zone, your learning zone. Deliberate practice stretches you beyond your comfort zone. Elite players get to higher and higher levels because they know how to push beyond what's easy. They understand the fundamentals of deliberate practice and have the drive and passion to endure the difficult early stages of learning a new skill, when making mistakes and failing is the norm.

In fact, to practice effectively, you must first experience failure. Failing isn't fun, but it is necessary in building new skills. After a disappointing practice, you must be willing to undertake the mentally, emotionally, and physically difficult process of working through the skill that, at the moment, seems just beyond your level. Growth comes through continuously pushing the edges of your comfort zone and working on skills that are just out of reach.

Do you want to know if you're working in the right zone? If you're messing up about half the time, then you're pushing past the edges of your comfort zone into the learning zone. If you're successful most of the time, then you're practicing in your comfort zone. The key is to find that sweet spot where something is challenging, but you can do it with hard work. That's where you want to focus your time and effort.

When I work with players, we talk about the three zones for practice and games and when to use each:

- **Comfort zone:** You feel comfortable, make few mistakes, and experience little discomfort. Your coaches are quiet or praising you, and you're successful in your skills and drills most of the time.

- **Learning zone:** You feel somewhat stressed, yet somewhat excited. You make a fair number of mistakes, and your coaches scream a little (or a lot, depending on the coach). Both you and your coach experience feelings of frustration, and you're not sure whether you can or should stick with it. (Many players quit trying before mastering the new skill.) And you only successfully execute a new skill about half the time.

- **Panic zone:** You feel massive stress, hear lots of yelling, and make many mistakes. You experience total frustration and struggle to do anything right. When you are successful, it's probably because you got lucky. Only the strong survive the panic zone.

The thing about these zones is they are all necessary if you want to move your game to the next level. The trick is to learn how and when to experience these different zones and what to expect when you're in them. If you want to be an elite player, you must be willing to experience each of these zones over and over, and do it in a balanced, deliberate manner. Let me explain.

Comfort Zone

The comfort zone is where many average players spend most of their time, but it can also be useful to the elite player. When the game is fast, intense, or on-the-line, you need to be able to go to a place within your skill set where you can perform consistently at a very high level. Coaches say, "Keep your game simple," during crunch time because they know that when you play a simple game, you're able to play with much more speed, intensity, and effectiveness because you're working in a familiar area where your skills are almost automatic.

Learning Zone

The learning zone trips up a lot of players. Why? Because they either venture into the learning zone at the *wrong time* (during a game) or fail to go there at the *right time* (during practice). Let me explain. The only way to expand your comfort zone is to work in the learning zone. This is where you push yourself and your ability to its limits. You try things you've never tried and do things you're not particularly good at.

It's not so far from your comfort zone that you feel at complete risk for failure, but you're sure to make mistakes, and that's where managing expectations comes into play. Like I've said, learning requires making mistakes. You know it and your coach knows it. But nobody likes making mistakes, so you're sure to get frustrated (and the coach is still going to yell). The trick is to stay in the learning zone, despite the frustration and the yelling. Manage your expectations and don't expect perfection or top performance while you learn.

For the most part, practice is when you'll want to spend more time in the learning zone. Remember, deliberate practice is where elite players are made. If you're not spending 50 percent or more of your time during practice in the learning zone, then you're losing valuable development time. A quality practice will require you to work both your strengths and weaknesses. Strengths typically live in your comfort zone and weaknesses in your learning zone. Push yourself to spend more time in the learning zone during practice so when it's game time, you're ready to use what you've learned. In games, however, it is better to simplify your game and excel in the areas where you are more confident so you can consistently perform at a high level.

Speed is important in elite hockey, and until you can execute a new skill with speed, it's a better idea to play fast and simple than to try things you're still learning. I'm not saying you'll never spend time in the learning zone during games because you will. It's inevitable. Hockey is a game of read and react, and you can't practice for mastery in every situation you will encounter. But if you keep your game simple and work to execute with speed and efficiency, then even these learning moments can be handled without disastrous results.

Panic Zone

The third zone, the panic zone, is the world of the unknown. It's big players moving really fast with skill and intensity that may feel beyond your current level. You'll recognize the panic zone because your heart will be pounding and your palms sweating. You will feel noticeably rattled. Everyone experiences the panic zone from time to time, but knowing what it is and how to use it to your advantage will give you an edge.

A good example of performing in the panic zone is when you're called up to play against players who are older, bigger, faster, and stronger, players who crush everything that moves. But, here's the thing about the panic zone: the panic zone is only the panic zone until it becomes the learning zone and then the comfort zone. That's how it works. Likewise, the first time you rode a bike you were probably freaking out. Now it's a breeze.

Try to retain the image of learning to ride a bike because when you're in the panic zone, you may forget how the process works and doubt yourself. You may think your mistakes mean you're not good enough and will never learn. Wrong! Managing your expectations when you're in the learning zone and panic zone is crucial. If you beat yourself up whenever you perform poorly, you're missing important opportunities to get better as a player.

This constant movement from comfort zone to learning zone to panic zone to learning zone to comfort zone, back and forth, back and forth, drives the process of deliberate practice forward. When practices aren't as effective as they should be, it is probably because players want to stay in their comfort zone. To improve, step outside of your comfort zone and work on areas of your game where you are weak, rather than practicing your strengths over and over.

Repetition

Deliberate practice requires repetition, repetition, repetition. Remember these words: *repetition builds strength*. The choice to practice deliberately is a choice you make every time you step on the ice. When you practice, you have a choice whether to use that time effectively or merely go through the motions. Deliberate practice is something elite players do every time they hit the ice to practice, and now that you understand, you must practice with purpose from this point forward.

I remember being at a junior practice where I watched a player at the end of practice (the best player on the team, I should mention). I watched as he headed to the half-wall area on the ice, dropped his gloves to use as

cones, and grabbed a puck. For the next ten minutes, he practiced puck handling along the boards, weaving in and out of the gloves, simulating tight coverage. With head up and feet flying, he used his body to protect the puck, keeping a high tempo and focused intensity.

After a few dekes, he would explode off the wall, drive the net, and lift the puck under the bar. Though he was already exhausted from a full practice, he did this drill no less that ten times, nobody on the ice but him— no coaches, no teammates, over and over and over. Today that player is in the NHL. His story is a great example of how repetition builds strength.

Game-Like Conditions

Deliberate practice means practicing under game-like conditions. When you first learn a skill, you break it down into its basic elements and move through each slowly and purposefully; however, to be effective, you eventually need to practice skills in game-like conditions, at game-like speed, and with game-like intensity.

Shaun Clouston, former head coach of the WHL Medicine Hat Tigers, shared his philosophy of practicing at game speed. He said, "If you're not practicing at game speed and intensity, then you're just wasting your time and mine." Kevin Constantine, coach of the WHL Everett Silvertips, said he would "kick players off the ice if they dialed it back in practice." Craig Laughlin, NHL veteran, hockey TV analyst, and coach of elite teams in the Mid-Atlantic, told me, "The best players I've ever coached always skate at game speed."

Hockey is a fast game, and game speed is typically faster than practice speed. It is important that you make a conscious effort to practice with game-like speed so you will be able to "bring it" at game time. The best coaches know that the teams that practice with speed and intensity play games at a level above their competition. Playoff games are even faster and more intense than regular season games. Have you ever wondered why a team can dominate in the regular season but fall short in the playoffs? One of the reasons is that they didn't adapt to the increased speed and intensity of the playoffs and probably got knocked out early.

To maximize your use of deliberate practice, you must accept it will be difficult. You will make a lot of mistakes, and learning is hard. But without these challenges, you will not be able to fine-tune your skills to achieve the elite performance you are hoping for. Becoming a gritty player requires resilient learning through trial and error.

Here are the eight steps to increase your grit through deliberate practice:

1. Try something.
2. Mess up.
3. Learn from your mistake.
4. Make adjustments.
5. Try again.
6. Mess up again, but hopefully less this time.
7. Try again and continue to evaluate, adapt, and adjust by observing your results and learning from your mistakes.
8. Never quit.

Screwing up and making mistakes is the key to focused, deliberate practice. There isn't a hockey player alive who hasn't made plenty of mistakes along the way. This is an important distinction. Mistakes, failure, frustration, difficulty, and adversity are *essential* aspects of deliberate practice. Perfectionism and fear of failure will derail your attempts to practice with a purpose and must be eliminated.

Now that you understand how deliberate practice can bring grit to your game, let's talk about how to alternate intensity and effort with rest and recovery periods to ensure a proper balance in your overall development.

Understand Effort, Overload, and Recovery

This next tip is extremely important if you wish to make the most of your practice time. It's a fundamental concept that, if ignored or misunderstood, will result in difficulty, hardship, pain, and dissatisfaction. Failure to understand recovery will prevent you from reaching the elite levels in hockey and can ultimately damage your love for the game.

Deliberate practice is very demanding. The level of intensity and mental focus required can quickly lead to exhaustion. Consistently pushing yourself beyond your physical and mental capacities can result in loss of motivation, physical and mental exhaustion, and a drop in your overall effectiveness.

Research suggests that the upper limit for deliberate practice is around sixty minutes at a time and a total of around four hours a day. Surprisingly, it isn't our physical abilities that limit the effectiveness of deliberate practice but rather the stress it puts on our mental capacities. Repeating over and over a skill we're just learning (or not very good at) isn't much fun, so it is important to try and stick to sixty-minute blocks to optimize your effort and help you get the most out of practice.

"Effort," in simple terms, is anything that causes energy to be expended. "Overload" is anything that causes you to work beyond what feels normal and move out of your comfort zone. It's when you try something new or difficult that pushes you beyond what you normally do. "Recovery" is the period of rest following the overload task. It's where you rest and recapture expended energy.

Physical overload occurs when you're on the ice during a game or practice. It's the physical movements of your muscles and body. As you work, your muscles expend energy, allowing you to perform. The more energy stored in your muscles, the better the performance level. That is why you train. When you train, you increase the amount of energy your muscles can store, which increases what they are able to expend; the more energy, the better the performance.

Mental overload occurs when you experience negative emotions, such as frustration, doubt, fear, anxiety, anger, jealousy, worry, depression, etc. These negative emotions drain you of energy and make you weaker.

The balance between effort and recovery is about the management of energy expended and energy recovered. It is easier to recognize expended physical energy than expended mental energy. When you have a strong shift and come back to the bench tired, you know you expended physical energy and understand needing a minute or two for your body to recover before you go back out. However, it's not quite as apparent when you expend mental energy, and it's even less apparent how to recover from the loss. So, let's look at two examples of effort and recovery: one physical and the other mental.

Physical Example: Power Skating Drills during Practice

When you first start the skating drill, your legs are fresh and strong. Your mind is clear and your focus is on execution. After a few minutes of high-intensity skating, your legs begin to tire and you start to slow down. To keep up your speed and intensity, you will need to rest between drills. It's really that simple. When you're tired, you're slower, and until you rest, you won't be able to go fast again.

Mental Example: Power Skating Drills during Practice

Your first reaction when the coach calls for the skating drills is frustration and irritation. You think, *I hate these drills!* You bang your stick and sulk to the line to start. You start off strong because you're fresh, but soon you're counting how many more reps you have left. You lose focus, and your execution becomes sloppy. Right about then, the coach starts riding you, telling you to "pick it up." Now you're tired *and* irritated.

You try to dig deep, but you're frustrated and tired. When you do try harder, all it does is cause you to tighten up. By the end of the drill, you're both mentally and physically exhausted. You know how to recover physically (take a rest), but how do you recover mentally? After all, you're pretty frustrated, and practice is just getting started.

In these two examples, stress was at a high level. In the first, the overload was mainly physical. Powerful strides and strong edges combined to expend physical energy. In the second, strides and edges were also a factor, but the negative attitude and emotions caused mental exhaustion as well.

In the physical example, a simple rest between drills is enough to recover and be ready to go again. However, in the second example, resting your muscles isn't enough to recover from the mental overload. And when you combine mental effort with physical effort, you lose energy *faster* because of the combined effort.

Unless you know how to recover from mental overload, you'll start from a depleted mental baseline when you hit the ice again. In other words, when your mental resolve is a little weaker, you will keep getting weaker, shift by shift, drill by drill. How long do you think you can go if each time out you are more and more exhausted? From a physical standpoint, you'll know. Your legs will feel like rubber and your strength and speed will disappear. But what happens when you exhaust your mental game?

This is when your emotions start to get the better of you. You begin to get frustrated or angry. You lose focus and struggle to keep your mind set on what you need to be doing. Your performance begins to drop off, and, pretty soon, the coach is riding you, or you find you aren't getting any more shifts. Being mentally tough is being able to  control and manage the expenditure of mental energy. It's recognizing the negative emotions that will eventually deplete you and replacing them with positive emotions that allow you to recover faster.

It's crucial to recognize and manage mental overload. If you are often frustrated, angry, and unable to focus, this could be a sign you are overtraining. On the other hand, too much recovery time can lead players to undertrain, which leaves you unprepared to play to your potential.

Managing effort and recovery for optimal training is a balancing act, so let's now determine the signs of over- and undertraining.

Signs of Over- and Undertraining

The signal for both overtraining and undertraining is discomfort and pain. Why? Because if you're not working hard enough to put your body in an ideal performance state, then you will fall behind physically and you'll need to train harder, or overtrain, to catch up. The most common signs of both over- or undertraining are inconsistency in your play and playing below your potential. The following chart lists other signs of over- or undertraining.

The Connection between Physical and Mental Stress

Physical	Mental
Chronic fatigue	Boredom
Muscle aches	Frustration
Frequent injury	Negative thoughts
Illness	Lack of focus
Pain	Lack of motivation
Changes in appetite	Mental errors

Physical and mental stress are clearly linked. Excessive physical stress leads to mental and emotional problems, and vice versa. Low energy, fatigue, and lack of motivation are often the body's way of signaling that it is overstressed, with insufficient recovery periods.

Is there such a thing as the perfect amount of effort? Of course. And that perfect amount is balanced with the right amount of recovery. When you train, you need to work yourself hard enough to grow both physically and emotionally. However, you must work smart so that you don't overload your mind and body to the point of shutdown.

If you want to increase your energy capacity, then you need to push the edges of your current capabilities. You've heard the saying, "no pain, no gain." It's true. But learning to recognize the right amount of training your body needs will help you avoid overdoing it while, at the same time, getting the most out of each workout. It's a balancing act: effort-recovery, effort-recovery.

These are the fundamentals of a solid training program. And as we make our bodies bigger, stronger, and faster, it's important to remember the same thing is happening in our mental game. Effort and overload are essential to physical and mental toughness. So is recovery. Push yourself, but listen to your body—and your thoughts and emotions—to know when to push harder and when to back off.

You'll recognize your physical growth through sore muscles and strength gained over time. You'll recognize your mental growth through an increased capacity to handle frustration, anger, and disappointment— the emotional ups and downs in hockey.

Understanding effort, overload, and recovery will allow you to balance your energy expenditure with energy recovery. Elite players are not endless supplies of energy; rather, they are players who have learned to manage their energy cycles. They know that for every killer workout, they need to give their body time to recover. They also recognize that negative emotions drain the body of energy. To manage their emotions, they allow time for a full recovery of both mental and physical energy.

So, let's summarize what it will take to go from just practicing to practicing deliberately, with a clearly defined purpose:

- **Write precise stretch goals.** Write down all the goals you have for your game and then break them down into specific skills. For example, if your goal is to skate faster, what can you work on each practice to improve your speed? Edges, knee-bend, and leg-extension are all skating skills that will help you increase your speed. But if you aren't deliberately working on clearly defined goals every time you hit the ice, then how can you expect to improve in a consistent manner?

- **Focus on the right things when you practice.** What's the right thing? Well, that depends on what you want to improve. If it's skating faster, then make sure you're paying attention to the skills that help you skate fast. Being able to manage your focus during practice allows you to work on what the coach is asking from you as well as working on the skills you're deliberately committed to improving.

- **Pay attention to feedback.** This is where your coach comes into play. You need someone else to give you feedback on whether or not you are improving your performance. You can't do this by yourself. You need insight and feedback from people who can guide you toward getting better. Share your practice goals with your coach or assistant coach so they can give you support and motivation to overcome any setback or moments of procrastination or laziness.

- **Repetition, repetition, repetition.** Deliberate practice means doing it over and over, utilizing reflection and refinement skills as you go along. Through repetition you can slowly program the mental wiring that will allow you to execute these skills without having to consciously think about them.

- **Fail forward.** To practice effectively, you first must experience failure. Failing isn't fun, but it is the first step in building a new skill. After experiencing failure, you must be willing to undertake the mentally, emotionally, and physically difficult process of working through something that, at the moment, is just beyond

your skill level. Growth comes through continuously
pushing the edges of your comfort zone and working
on skills that are just beyond your reach.

Okay, so now you should be convinced that you need to take a good, hard look at your practice preparation and effectiveness. Use the skills we talked about in this chapter to improve the quality of your time in practice, so that you can get more out of your skills in games. It's not just about working harder. It's about working smarter. It's knowing what you want to work on, and then deliberately drilling these skills to get better and better.

Remember, mistakes and failure are to be expected when you're learning something new, so give yourself some room to experiment and be willing to screw up a little without getting down on yourself. Now, I can't promise you the coach won't give you some grief, but hang in there anyway.  When you use deliberate practice to improve as a player, the long-term benefit to your coach and your teammates will more than make up for the grief you may get. When you're able to perform at a high level when it counts the most, you'll know it was worth it.

Everything we have talked about so far demands effort: knowing yourself and your game requires honesty and openness; setting goals requires commitment and hard work. Likewise, changing how you practice and rest will require energy because you'll need to unlearn and relearn some important skills and strategies. You'll make mistakes. You'll screw up. You'll get frustrated. You'll probably get yelled at. Change like this is hard.

So, the question is, if it's so difficult, how do you hang in there when you're pushed to your limit? The answer is perseverance, a crucial element of grit and the subject of our next chapter.

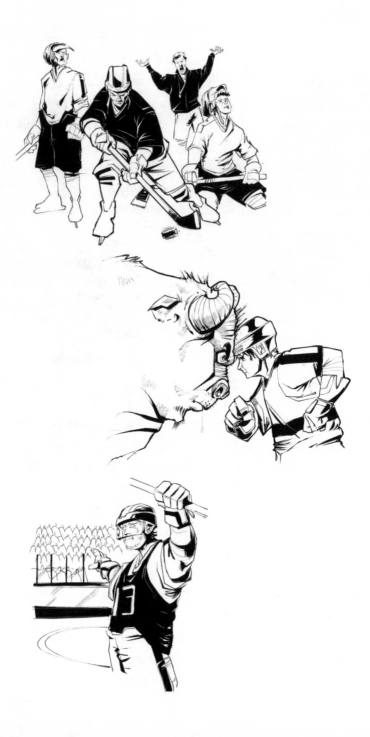

Chapter 6

Perseverance

With his heart thumping in his chest, Brendan looked up at the roster posted on the board to find out if he made the team. Having already been cut in four previous tryouts, Brendan was starting to wonder if he was going to make any team for the upcoming season.

As Brendan scanned down the list, his stomach dropped when he didn't see his name. Talking to the coaches about why he didn't make the team, Brendan heard the same thing: "You're a great player. You hustle; you battle; you make guys work for every chance they get; but you're just too small. Goalies today are six feet tall or more, and you just don't have the size. We're sorry, but we've decided to go with the other guys. Thanks for trying out."

Walking out of the rink, towing his bag behind him, Brendan knew he had one more shot. Sitting in the car, not even out of the parking lot,

Brendan registered for a supplemental tryout being held in a town three hours away.

Fast forward one week and Brendan finds himself getting ready to pull up the website with the names of the goalies picked in the last tryout of the season. With seven goalies at the supplemental tryouts and several of them tall dudes, Brendan knew the odds were against him. Taking a deep breath, he clicked enter to see the list. His name was at the top of the list. He made it.

Perseverance is what players use to consistently and continually progress toward their goals, despite the obstacles and adversity encountered along the way. Other terms used to describe perseverance are persistence, dedication, determination, doggedness, stamina, mettle, or tenacity—all these terms accurately describe this crucial component of grit.

Players with perseverance love to compete; they are in it for the long haul. They are always working to improve so they can dominate on the ice, and they consistently play with confidence, pride, and passion. Perseverance is the drive that keeps players moving toward their goals, despite setbacks and obstacles.

Not everyone can be 6′2″ and 220 pounds. Not everyone can skate like the wind or have a bomb from the point. But we can all practice our skills to get better, and perseverance will keep us going when things get difficult or challenging.

Some of the critical components of perseverance are the exact skills we've already discussed, such as setting goals and maintaining focus. A player who lacks meaningful goals is not likely to be focused or persistent in his pursuit of excellence. Likewise, a player with a negative attitude will be pessimistic about his ability to achieve success and is more likely to bail when things get tough. So, it is important to recognize that being a persistent, gritty, determined player means you must develop in all areas of your game—mental and physical.

Beyond hockey, perseverance is a character skill that will help you all throughout your life. Perseverance will help you earn good grades in school, establish a great reputation with coaches and scouts, and stay on the path toward the life goals you set for yourself.

On almost every team, it seems like there's that one guy who just works a little harder than everyone else. He's the one you see on the ice, working on skills before and after practice. He trains in the off-season. He spends a lot of his own time perfecting his game and seems to do well in pretty much every  other aspect of his life, too. He always seems focused and seldom messes around when there's work to be done.

What separates that guy from his teammates? Where does he find the energy and the willpower to make goal-oriented decisions that keep him moving in a straight path toward what he wants? Most important, is this discipline and self-control a skill you can learn?

The answer is a resounding yes! While people used to believe perseverance was something you either had or you didn't, research shows exactly the opposite. Perseverance is a skill you can learn to develop, and this chapter will teach you to grow the steadfast determination you need to go far in hockey. When you cultivate mental toughness, willpower, and resilience, you will build the kind of perseverance elite players possess. We will also discuss managing negative emotions and controlling your performance in a way that keeps you pushing forward, persevering against all odds, in every circumstance.

Develop Mental Toughness

Mental toughness is a critical component of grit and, thus, of perseverance. As such, it is one of the most important qualities elite players can acquire. Players who can get the job done and stay focused, despite distractions or emotions arising during competition, are the ones who have the most success. Players with strong, unwavering mindsets have a tremendous capacity to make the most of their talents and compete day in and day out at a high level.

Mental toughness is the ability to consistently perform at the top of your game, regardless of what is going on around you. So, what does this look like? The following concepts are key in understanding mental toughness:

- Mental *flexibility*: the ability to stay calm and centered in the face of adversity, stress, and emotional turmoil; the ability to summon positive emotions in the face of negative ones
- Mental *responsiveness*: the ability to respond in emotionally healthy ways to situations as they arise; to stay engaged and balanced under pressure
- Mental *strength*: the ability to withstand pressure and remain emotionally balanced
- Mental *resiliency*: the ability to recover quickly and bounce back after facing adversity, obstacles, and difficult situations

When considering how to develop your perseverance, think of these characteristics that distinguish players with mental toughness:

- They use toughness to maximize their talents and skills.
- They are focused, confident, emotionally strong, and instinctive.
- They are in control: mentally, emotionally, and physically.
- They continuously work to improve and develop their toughness.

Research shows that as players progress and teams and individuals are more evenly matched in skill and experience, it is the psychological factors—like mental toughness—that become the most important determinate of a player's success.

How Tough Are You?

It is a difficult thing to look at yourself and assess your mental toughness. To do so, you need to strip away your pride and take a good, hard, honest look at the real you. It can be scary to place yourself under a microscope; however, as we discussed in detail in chapter 3, honest self-assessment is a prerequisite to becoming a powerful and dedicated competitor.

By now, you should know your scores for four assessments: TAIS, the Complete Player Profile, HockeyType, and Grit Scale. Admittedly, much of what is revealed through assessments can be observed in a player's performance and development over time. However, observation alone can take a very long time. It is common for coaches to express astonishment at how much I can learn about a player, through these assessments, after having only worked with him for a few hours.

Player assessment tools, such as the TAIS, the Complete Player Profile, HockeyType, and Grit Scale, help you to understand, predict, and control behavior and are an excellent addition to other peak-performance coaching strategies.

Strengthen Your Weakest Links

If you were honest in your answers, your player assessment scores will show your areas of strength as well as areas you can improve. While it may be painful to look at those weaknesses, it is important to be aware. During the intensity of competition, we always break where we are the weakest. This is true whether the weak links are mental, emotional, or physical. To increase the mental toughness in your game, you need to focus your training on your areas of weakness.

You can't change what you don't acknowledge, so we worked on self-perception in chapter 3. With self-awareness, you can undergo mental training to strengthen the weak links, much as you would undergo physical training to strengthen a physical weakness. You can actually build perseverance, much in the same way you build muscle fiber.

If you have difficulty assessing yourself or seeing your weakness, seek feedback from those who know you best, and be open to what you learn. Mental toughness training is the path toward mastery and gaining a competitive edge.

No matter where you are with mental toughness right now, you can train yourself to become tougher, to dig deeper. It is a learned skill that takes work and practice, much like many of the other skills you develop as a hockey player. Mental toughness needs to be trained and practiced for you to become proficient.

Mental Toughness Training

Mental toughness training is about improving your attitude and mental-game skills. It helps you perform your best by identifying beliefs that limit you and taking a more positive and trusting approach toward your ability to play hockey at a high level.

Here is a list of the top ten ways mental toughness training can boost your skill, attitude, and performance:

1. **It improves focus to help you deal with distractions.** Many players have the ability to concentrate, but often their focus is placed on the wrong areas. For example, a player might think to himself, *I have to score today*, which is a results-oriented focus. Mental toughness training focuses on ways to maintain your focus on the present moment, the here and now, while letting go of worry about results. Worrying about results takes your mind away from the game and interferes with your play.

2. **It enhances player confidence and removes doubt.** Doubt is the opposite of confidence. If you have doubts prior to or during practices or games, you probably suffer from some degree of low confidence in one or more areas of your game. At a minimum, this doubt is sabotaging whatever confidence you had to start with. Confidence is a core mental-game skill and one we will talk about often.

3. **It provides you with skills to deal with mistakes and/or setbacks.** Emotional balance is a prerequisite to getting into the zone. Some players with strict expectations have trouble dealing with the normal mistakes that are a natural part of improving in hockey. It is important to address these expectations so that players can stay composed when they feel pressure, make mistakes, or become frustrated.

4. **It allows you to find the right zone of intensity when you play.** I use "intensity" in a broad sense to identify the level of energy, arousal, or mental activation that is necessary for you to play your best, and this level will vary from player to player. Feeling pumped up

and positively charged is extremely important, but one must guard against getting overly excited. The best players are able to fine-tune their intensity to maximize their game. The goal is to be able to ride the fine line between being psyched up and being psyched out.

5. **It will help you and your teammates improve communication and team unity.** An important part of mental toughness training is helping teams improve bonding and communication with each other. The more a team works as a unit, the stronger the team will be and the better the results will be on the ice.

6. **It instills a healthy belief system and helps you identify irrational thoughts.** One of the areas where mental toughness training is so powerful is in helping players identify ineffective beliefs and attitudes (such as comfort zones and negative self-talk) that hold them back from performing well. These unhealthy core beliefs need to be identified and replaced with a new, healthier way of thinking. Unhealthy or irrational beliefs will keep you stuck at a lower level—no matter how much you practice or how hard you try.

7. **It improves motivation for optimal performance.** It is important to look at your level of motivation and understand *why* you play hockey. Some motivators are better in the long term than others. Players who are externally motivated can sometimes play for the wrong reasons, such as the player who only participates in hockey because of a coach or parent. Mental toughness training will help players adopt a healthy level of motivation and to be motivated for the right reasons, such as "develop my skills to play NCAA or major

junior" or "become a top-six forward on my team" or "have a top goals-against-average in the league."

8. **It provides critical postinjury confidence.** Some players find themselves fully prepared physically to get back into competition and practice, but on a mental level, scars can still remain. An injury can hurt confidence, generate doubt, and cause a lack of focus. Mental toughness training helps players heal mentally from injuries and cope with the fear of reinjury.

9. **It lets you develop game-specific strategies and plans.** All great coaches employ game plans to help players mentally prepare for practice and games. Mental toughness goes beyond basic mental skills and puts you in the company of the best players in the game.

10. **It helps you identify and enter the "zone" more often.** Being "in the zone" incorporates many of the key elements of mental toughness training in hockey. You're not going to play in the zone every day, but when you become mentally tough, you set the conditions for this to happen more often.

Strengthen Willpower

Another facet of perseverance is willpower, the ability to restrain our impulses and stay the course. When we think of willpower, we often see it as a do or don't proposition. Do we have the willpower to get up every day during the summer and run before the day gets too hot? Or do we have the willpower not to eat fast food during the season to keep our energy high and our bodies fit?

Think of willpower as the power of yes and the power of no. The power of yes is the ability to choose habits and behaviors that will move you forward in pursuit of your goals. For example, getting up half an hour early to exercise or showing up to practice forty-five minutes early to work on your skills.

The power of no is the ability to say no to something that falls outside of your goals. For many athletes, the power of no is applied to behaviors and choices that can derail your hockey career: drinking, smoking, drugs, poor eating habits, and poor sleeping habits.

There's one more power in willpower I want to mention because it is consistent with our discussion of perseverance, purpose, and passion: the power of want. The power of want is your ability to focus on what you want in the long term, rather than what you want in the moment. For example, turning off your alarm and going back to sleep gives you the short-term gratification of getting more sleep. While this may seem like the option you most want in the moment, if you focus firmly on your goal of becoming a better hockey player, you will benefit over the long term by getting up and working out. You tap into your willpower to stay committed to your long-term goals when faced with short-term pleasure.

In short, willpower is the single-minded drive, the unshakable resolve that is fundamental to perseverance. And, as I've mentioned, self-discipline and an "I can" attitude up your game and compensate for inherent weaknesses. Unlike natural talent or genetics, willpower is something you control and strengthen. Use it to your full advantage.

Foster Resilience

Resilience is the ability to bounce back and get in a positive mental space after a setback—a disappointing loss, a bad game, or harsh feedback from the coach. As you move up the ranks in hockey, you'll find that resiliency, or what I call "bounce," is an important part of perseverance. Developing bounce is critical if you want hockey to be part of your life for years to come.

Players who are resilient feel like they have a strong sense of control over their game and their outcome. A lack of resiliency almost always stems from the belief that you have no control, that your story is left to fate. While you may not be able to control what other people do or say, you can control yourself. Let me say that again. While you may not be able to control every situation life throws at you, you can always control your response to those situations.

When an obstacle or major setback occurs or when you face adversity, you get to decide how to respond to the situation. You get to choose how you'll think, react, and feel. You ultimately choose what you will do about it. It's a power we sometimes forget we have, but you do have the power to persevere. You can choose resilience, dig in your heels, and focus on how to get back on track.

When you experience a setback, instead of looking at yourself as a victim, consider it a challenge. Think of some adversity or setback you've experienced in hockey. How did you respond? Did you feel like you had any control in the situation? Did you step up to the challenge, stick with it, and keep  going, or did you bail? And if you did bail, why? How might have you stepped up instead?

You always have a choice in every situation. No matter what comes up, there are choices. I'm not saying you will always like the available choices, but you still have the power to choose. It's not what happens to you that determines where you go; it's how you respond to what happens to you that decides your future. This is one of those Zen-like ideas that can change the way you look at your life.

Think about resilient people you know—players or coaches or family members who are tough to their core and don't seem to let anything get in their way. You can have that same energy and relentless persistence if you remember you have control over your response and resilience.

A Parable of Perseverance

Everybody responds to adversity differently. Again, your individual traits, what you want, and what you believe about yourself are all factors affecting how you respond. Two common responses to adversity I see in players can be summarized through players I'll call Mr. Easy and Mr. Intensity.

Mr. Easy looks as if he is putting in the effort, but in reality, he is probably only working as hard as the coach expects him to. He typically spends more time working on the skills and areas of his game where he's already good. He may put in some off-ice time but only enough to get by. And during his time in the gym, he's not pushing himself.

Mr. Easy might be an incredible player, or he might be an average player; it all depends on his natural athletic ability. But one thing is for sure: Mr. Easy will quickly figure out the minimum level of effort he can get away with and then settle in that groove until something forces him to change.

In contrast, Mr. Intensity is a worker who competes like a boss, even when the coach isn't watching. He logs extra hours in the gym and on the ice. He communicates well with the coach to understand his role and the expectations others have for him. He's a good teammate and pushes his teammates to work hard and give their best all of the time. He's always looking for ways to improve his game, and whenever he feels like he's leveling out, he'll find something to challenge himself.

An interesting thing happens when each of these players experiences adversity. Mr. Easy usually tries to avoid the difficult situation. He may become frustrated and angry, or he may just give up. Mr. Intensity, on the other hand, takes it as a serious challenge. When he encounters difficulty, he takes his play up another notch, becoming focused on what it will take to overcome the challenge. He is committed to moving past whatever difficulty he encountered to carry on.

You can be sure that both players will experience difficulty and adversity in the process of playing hockey. The difference is, Mr. Intensity will respond with perseverance and work through challenges with deliberate focus, effort, and intensity. He will be resilient. Mr. Easy will freeze and then either avoid the difficult situation or make excuses. Mr. Easy just doesn't understand the importance of determination, resilience, and willpower.

Manage Negative Emotions

Another important factor in perseverance is the ability to manage your emotions. We talked about the role emotions play in mental exhaustion and overload; now, let's consider the role of emotion in developing mental toughness, an important factor in our ability to stay the course. If we want to endure and become elite competitors, we must be the master of our emotions.

Did you know that your emotions have an effect on your physiology? It's true. Extreme emotions affect breathing, blood flow, muscle control, and more. In the face of extreme negative emotions, our ability to control our bodies and focus on the physical requirements of the game is compromised. In contrast, mental focus and physical precision are maximized when you've trained yourself to be mentally tough.

In emotionally charged situations, where you tend to want to give up, you must manage the negative emotion and learn to "respond with challenge." To respond with challenge means you become emotionally engaged, confident, positive, and full of fight when faced with a difficult situation. Sometimes, a challenge response may come naturally to you. Other times, you may struggle to stay positive.

It's tempting, when faced with discouragement or disappointment, to go negative. Instead of maintaining confidence and doubling down, we can give way to anger, anxiety, or fear. Players with mental toughness learn to tame these negative emotions and come out on top, proving their elite status by the way they handle themselves on the ice. To persevere, it is important to recognize negative emotional states, learn to calm yourself, and bring your focus back to the game. Let's now explore some of the emotions you are likely to experience during a game.

Negative Emotions Sabotage Your Game

Anger

Some believe getting angry is a great way to increase motivation and competitive performance. You may be surprised, however, to learn that while anger might spur intensity, it is not an effective long-term motivator for elite performance. Anger is a common emotional response and what psychologists consider a negative emotion. It disrupts the ideal performance state by affecting focus and composure, two critical mental skills elite players must have.

Players who experience anger can direct it inward (negative thoughts and negative self-talk) or outward (bad penalty; fighting; mouthing off to a teammate, coach, or ref). All of these reactions are damaging to performance, so why would players give in to anger? Some use it to control their nerves; to self-protect; to cover deeper, less acceptable emotions (shame, doubt, sadness); or to increase intensity.

To defeat anger, players must recognize it in themselves and then admit that it is undermining their game. Negative energy generated by anger should not be used as a motivator as it flares up quickly and burns out fast. Anger can also camouflage weightier emotions that must be resolved for forward motion with hockey and life. Ask yourself, *Is my anger actually an expression of self-doubt or shame? Does my surface anger signal a deeper need?*

Anxiety

Choking is falling short of your capabilities; it can be a devastating experience for a player—but it can be avoided if you understand the emotions underpinning the event. Choking is usually brought about by self-doubt and anxiety.

Remember, even the best players choke from time to time. In fact, it's a sign that something is important to you and you care a great deal about the outcome. You get anxious because you're passionate about what you're doing and want to be the best.

If you don't choke now and again, chances are, you aren't pushing hard enough; players who never choke may be unengaged. But mentally tough hockey players learn to handle intense situations in a way that prevents them from screwing up their head or their game.

If you want to persevere in anxiety-provoking circumstances, you must gain control over your doubt. Confidence is the enemy of choking and the antidote for doubt. The more confidence you have in your ability to deliver, the less likely you are to choke. The more you worry about choking, the more likely you will choke.

If you do choke, your goal is to stay focused on the game and available to your teammates. Resolve to set aside negative emotion and bring your intensity back to the game by focusing on two or three specific hockey skills that help you play your best. Go back to basics and simplify. Choking occurs when you overthink the situation or worry you don't have the experience and composure to handle it. Setting your mind on a few select process skills (battling for the puck, backchecking, or keeping your feet moving) allows your mind to focus on less, allowing your body to do what it knows how to do without letting your thoughts get in the way.

Choking because of panic or inexperience must be resolved through practice and expanding situations you will face in pressure moments. This kind of choke is resolved with more practice whereas the other kind of choke is resolved by proper focus.

Discouragement

This chapter is dedicated to the importance of perseverance. No one makes it to the elite level by giving up, so why have I seen talented players quit? The main reason players bail is because they fear failing or falling short of expectations. For some players, failing is so painful that they would rather not try, so they use their lack of effort as the excuse for a poor performance.

They rationalize their failure by not going all-in, not giving their best; then, they can soothe themselves by remembering they didn't really try. In reality, these players are discouraged; they are down on themselves, unsure they have what it takes. Rather than know for certain, they hold back and hide behind a lack of effort. They play without heart to protect their heart.

Discouraged players may never know what they are truly capable of achieving. It's like they're riding around with their foot on the brake, afraid to take it off. Discouragement and the disengagement it produces derail more players than almost any other mental weakness. Disengagement does reduce your immediate pain; however, it has another, unwanted effect. It keeps you from reaching your full potential as a player. When you allow discouragement to take over, you withdraw your emotional energy from the game, causing your performance mechanisms to shut down. It is impossible to disengage emotionally without withdrawing physically.

Giving up is always followed by excuse making, which frequently leads to refusing responsibility for the results. Perhaps you've heard—or made—some of the following excuses:

- I could have done better, if I wanted to—I just wasn't feeling it today.
- I never play my best against this team or at this rink.
- No matter how hard I play, nothing changes; so, why bother?

Each of these statements excuse the player from trying, often placing the blame elsewhere. The next time you catch yourself bailing, ask yourself, *Can anyone really make me behave in a certain way? When I chose to disengage from the situation, was it someone else's fault?*

The answer to both of these questions is, of course, no. You made the choice to give in to the negative feelings of discouragement. We may tell ourselves we're being forced out or have no choice but to give up, but that's not true. It's always up to you.

You alone can battle your negative feelings. You alone are responsible for your response to each circumstance in your life. Therefore, you alone are ultimately responsible for every controllable outcome. This realization can be extremely empowering.

The way to avoid discouragement and disengagement is to "step up" to the challenges that typically cause you to withdraw. Instead of withdrawing to protect your ego, lean into the test. Realize that you are in control of your response to the situation and have the power to persevere.

Fear

Ultimately, the root of negative emotions—including anger, anxiety, and discouragement—is fear. While there are many ways you can respond, you must choose to fight back and remain in control of your mental game. Your main weapon for combating fear is the ability to step up and challenge the situation. When fear, in any form, rears its ugly head, *step up, engage, and meet it head-on.*

See the imperfect situation as a challenge; harness your fear and use the power of this emotion to get fired up. Fear is inevitable, but strong players know they have a choice about how fear affects their game. Choose to manage your negative emotions like a champion.

You are in control of your emotions. You can choose your response and change the outcome of difficult situations. If you really believed this, how would your behavior in challenging circumstances change—both on and off the ice? Would you spend your energy on negative responses, which lead to increased pain and potentially negative outcomes, or would you use your energy to respond positively, meet the challenge head-on, and ultimately grow as a player?

Throughout this book and by utilizing the Complete Player Coaching Program, you are learning grit. Sure, you might experience negative emotion now and again, but with every failure come the seeds of an equal or greater opportunity. With every difficult circumstance comes the chance to prove your perseverance. So, gather your confidence, master your emotion, and go for it!

Become a Performer

When it comes to hockey, it's challenging to compete at a high level day in and day out. Sometimes you feel electric; things just click. But, what about times of struggle? What happens when you have a game or practice and, for whatever reason, your energy is low, your focus is off, and you're just not feeling it? You probably know what I am talking about, and the universality of this experience is one reason we are learning about perseverance. You have to know how to keep going when part of you wants to give up.

Get to Know the Two Sides of You

Did you know you have two sides to your personality? You do. In fact, you bring out one or the other each time you play hockey (or do anything for that matter). You have the "real" you, your true self, how you really think and feel, but it's probably not someone you show others often. That self can feel tired, stressed, frustrated, worried, scared, or angry and lacks confidence now and again. Many times, how you really feel isn't going to help you carry on when the going gets rough. That's why you need to know about the other you.

The "performer" you is the person you need to be to play your best. It's the suit of armor you put on to bring it when the real you doesn't feel it. This performer in you calls forth positive feelings and emotions, allowing you to play with confidence and focus and to perform consistently in the upper range of your skill and talent.

When you have grit, you are able to call upon the performer when negative thoughts, feelings, and emotions threaten to interfere with your performance. Accessing the performer inside allows you to keep going when circumstances threaten to sidetrack the real you.

Preparing to Persevere

The performer who perseveres has readied himself in practice and understands how to control his mental game when negative emotions hit. The following list summarizes the preparation necessary to perform at the elite level:

- **Physical preparation.** Physical preparedness includes being well rested, getting adequate sleep, being properly hydrated, and eating the right kind of fuel to perform in a peak state.

- **Emotional preparation.** Emotional preparedness comes from positive self-worth and high confidence. With these core values in place, it is much easier to overcome temporary negative emotions.
- **Hockey sense and game skills.** Having hockey sense and skills means practicing and solidifying the fundamentals of the game so that skill performance becomes automatic.
- **Physical toughness.** Elements of physical toughness include muscular strength and a tolerance for all types of discomfort, including exhaustion and pain. A physically tough player hits the wall but plays through.

Accessing the Performer You

Human beings respond emotionally to internal and external stimuli. During a game, the way that you feel (the real you) and the way you *need* to feel to enter into your ideal performance state may be vastly different. When this happens, you need to access the performer in you to play your best. You must learn to act "as if."

Utilizing your performer skills means you become an actor. If you aren't feeling confident and invincible, then act like you do. If you are feeling tired but you need to appear energetic and alert, act energetic and alert. Your body will follow suit. If, on the other hand, you give in to negativity and hang your head or drop your shoulders, your game will follow in a downward spiral. Allowing your outer behaviors to reflect inner negative feelings is a big problem if you want to persevere and fight.

When you act on negative feelings, you not only reinforce those emotions, but you also cause them to accelerate. When you're feeling angry or anxious and you let those feelings show by yelling or slamming your stick, then your anger and anxiety win. Acting "as if" is the strategy

Complete Players use as their first and best line of defense to manage problematic emotions.

Research shows that the body reacts physiologically in the same way to fake emotion as it does to genuine emotion. So, if you aren't feeling up to par, fake the emotions you need to have—confidence, energy, relaxed mental state, etc.—and your body will soon follow.

Imagine being in a game and feeling frustrated about a call that didn't go your way. You need to call upon your performer self to manage your frustration. So, how do you access grit and move forward with a positive attitude when you just aren't feeling it? Try this. First, fix your thoughts on how it feels to be steadfast and committed. Next put a cold, steely, determined stare on your face. Hold your head up, keep your back straight, clench your jaw, and see yourself as a warrior ready for battle. That's it; you are now in a state of grit and determination.

You can call upon your performer skills at any time by following these tips:

- Use both disciplined thought and imagination. Keep your mind directed at the emotions you are trying to achieve. Imagine yourself feeling the emotions that you wish to show.
- Focus on having your body display the emotion you are trying to achieve. Adjust your posture, facial expressions, and movements to mimic the emotions you wish to convey.

- Practice emotional responses. During your time away from the ice, prtice the emotions you want to call upon as performer skills. This practice makes it easier to access these emotions during intense moments of play.
- Fill out the THINK Tough and ACT Tough charts below to prepare for these tough moments. I got you started with a couple examples.

Think Tough

If you're feeling . . .	Try thinking . . .
Like nothing is going your way in the game	*Example: Hold on and fight! The tide is turning in our direction.*
Afraid, stressed, or worried	*Example: I can do this! I love this.*
Exhausted and burned out	
Like giving up	
Frustrated or angry	

Act Tough

If you're feeling . . .	Try acting . . .
Exhausted and unable to push through	*Example: Energetic. Skate quickly. Keep an alert body posture.*
Like you just screwed up	*Example: With confidence only. Head up. Shoulders back*
Panicked	
Like you are choking	
Disappointed	

Beware of the Pretender!

The ability to tap into your performer self when you need to step up is an important part of your hockey development. That being said, it is important that you only access your performer self when you need to. In other words, you don't want to become this "false" person, faking everything you do. Acting like a warrior when you don't feel like a warrior is important for going through the wall when you need too, but acting like someone you are not in your everyday life can cause you to lose who you really are. Honesty about who you are and what you can do is enhanced when you learn how to access your performer self, but if you become a pretender, you will disconnect from reality and your development and performance will suffer.

Juggling your true self with your performer self is an important balance. Most of the time, your true self is who you need to be. Only when you are struggling and need to increase your grit should you tap into the performer side, which will enable you to step up and play your best.

In the next chapter, I want to circle back around to passion, where we first started. The foremost motivating factor in hockey—as in every sport—is a passion for the game. Passion is the fuel that helps you endure when things are difficult. As we come back to passion, let's talk about the aspects of passion that will keep you on the path to your dreams. Unlike external motivation, this internal fire will give you reason to keep going when times are difficult.

Chapter 7

Passion to Stay

Brett is completely wiped. He stayed up to half past two in the morning to put the finishing touches on the paper due today. It will be a full day, starting with a morning workout and team meeting before class. After class, he'll board the team bus to head north for two games against the top team in the league. The four-hour bus ride might be a good chance to catch up on homework and prepare for his final exam —that is, if he can keep his eyes open.

With only four hours' sleep, Brett is feeling run down, but he knows he better find some energy. If the team gets swept this weekend, they'll miss the playoffs and the season will be over.

The team splits the weekend set and now their fate will be up to the other teams' performance. On the bus ride back, Brett ices a sore groin and badly bruised forearm while balancing his psych book on his knee and trying to study for his finals on Monday.

Looking out the window at the houses whizzing by, Brett asks himself, *Why am I killing myself like this?* But then a smile comes to his face as he sees his reflection in the glass, and he quietly says to himself, *Because I love this game.* He then shouts the realization for everyone else to hear: "I love this stupid game!" Several of his teammates look around as Brett just sits there with a smile on his face. He says it again, "I love this game."

This is a true story about a player I worked with during his senior year as he was playing D1 hockey in the Midwest. Brett isn't his real name, but his challenges, his frustrations, and his passion are real.

Brett knew how tough playing hockey could be; he'd been living it for sixteen years. To keep going, with all the pressures building up as he neared the end of his college career—including classes, papers, finals, and, of course, battling to make the playoffs—passion was essential. At the end of the day, in the quietness of his own mind, Brett knew his love for the game had never wavered through the long, hard battle that is hockey. As difficult as it was some days to do it all, he still had a burning passion for the game. That's what makes hockey so special. No matter how exhausting the journey, the love of the game can still remain.

At the beginning of this book, I shared with you how passion is the spark that put you on the path toward achieving success in hockey. I also hinted at another aspect of passion that might be even more important than the initial excitement: passion to stay the course.

Passion is a powerful force in hockey and something to recognize if you want to go far. In this chapter, we will talk about several aspects of passion that can keep you motivated and inspired to persist, even when things are difficult or uncertain.

How would you assess your level of passion for the game right now? Is it as strong as it was when you first started? Stronger? Do you have the kind of passion that will push you to do whatever it takes to be the best?

Many players I work with ooze passion for hockey in everything they do. Other players admit that they had it once, but are not so sure now. Others, sadly, have lost their passion all together and have either dropped out of the game or are playing without the spark they once had. I cannot overstate how important passion is to the game of hockey. It is the only hope for weathering the trials and tribulations you'll face in becoming an elite player.

To understand the impact passion can have on your game, we must consider how optimism, enthusiasm, and gratitude affect the commitment and dedication required to play and love this game—even when times are tough.

Optimism

Research shows that optimists outperform pessimists in every area of life, including school, work, social interactions, and sports. Therefore, optimism has become an integral part of peak performance training and mental-game coaching. Optimists are more hopeful about their future and, as a result, train more effectively, perform more consistently, and handle setbacks better than pessimists.

Optimists enjoy greater success as they are more engaged in their efforts and have positive feelings and high expectations about their future. Experience shows that optimistic players bounce back from setbacks more quickly, are less likely to choke under pressure, and develop more quickly and consistently than others.

Optimism has two components: expectations and explanations. In their book *Performing under Pressure*, Weisinger and Pawliw-Fry define "expectations" as how you think about the future and "explanations" as how you describe the past.[7] Earlier, we explored types and sources of expectations, but it is worth noting that optimists have a specific kind of expectation. Optimistic players expect to have success in what they do, whether it's in practice or in games. They have a fundamental sense that things will work out and go their way.

This positive mindset not only boosts player confidence, but it also has a huge impact on how a player will react to the inevitable pressure and adversity hockey brings. Optimists feel less anxiety and stress and are willing to push their skills and abilities, allowing them to develop quickly and play at the upper end of their talent in pressure situations.

The second element of optimism is how you look back on and describe your experiences. Positive players describe past setbacks and adversity as opportunities for learning. Rather than getting discouraged and frustrated during hard times, they remain persistent and don't give up under pressure the way negative players do. Think back to some of the difficult times you've had in hockey and ask yourself, *Did I look at these difficulties as an opportunity for learning, or was I frustrated, wanting it to just be over?* Likewise, think of preparing for a big game against a tough opponent and ask, *Did I feel excited and nervous, or did I feel anxiety and dread?*

Optimism changes how we feel about our future and the stories we tell about our past. Positive players are able to roll with the punches. Knowing that negative times are temporary, they play with more focus, composure, and determination. Optimistic players are also more resilient and persistent, able to bounce back after adversity. All of these characteristics give optimists a noticeable advantage over players with a negative mindset.

Research shows that being positive and optimistic creates energy that can be used by both the individual and the people around him. Ever wonder why you feel so hyper and energized when you're with other positive people? Likewise, being around pessimism and negativity is a huge energy drain.

Think back to a time when a coach ripped the team on the bench or threw a nutty in practice. Did that energize you or exhaust you? If you're like most players I work with, a negative teammate or coach can suck the energy right out of the room. At times when you need a boost, their negative energy takes the wind right out of your sails.

While optimism is important to a player's performance, it's important to note there can be a negative effect if optimism isn't balanced with reality. Too much optimism can lead to overconfidence, excessive risk-taking, and a lack of awareness of important performance cues, all of which can ultimately result in a negative situation rather than a positive one.

Take, for instance, players who are overly optimistic; they are so sure they will make an all-star team they don't give their full effort, assuming it's already in the bag. Or consider a goalie who has a shutout going against a team that has never won against his team; he skates out to play the puck, something he never does, and ends up getting beat on the play. Confidence, boldness, and optimism are all excellent traits for an elite player, but they must be balanced with a grasp of reality. You must avoid being overly optimistic to the point of taking ill-advised risks or overlooking the facts of the situation.

Enthusiasm

Pumped. Excited. Jazzed. Energized. These are the words that define "enthusiasm." It is a heightened state of arousal, an invisible boost of positive energy that is difficult for opposing teams to defeat. To me, enthusiasm and positive energy go hand in hand. Players who play positive, energized hockey are playing with enthusiasm.

Enthusiasm may be one of the most underappreciated team attributes, but its impact on performance can be the difference between a successful season and an unsuccessful one. I've seen teams laden with talent dramatically underachieve because of a lack of enthusiasm. In contrast, I've seen teams put together with average players excel beyond anyone's wildest expectations, all because of enthusiasm.

From a psychological standpoint, enthusiasm is a way for individuals and teams to motivate their desires, deepen their engagement, and develop their interests. It can unlock creativity, build team cohesion, and develop individual and team resilience. When talking about maintaining your passion in hockey, enthusiasm cannot be left out of the equation.

Enthusiasm is both mental and physical. Positive self-talk and positive expectations can energize individual players to perform at levels beyond their current skill. Enthusiastic players skate with a spring in their step and pounce on pucks like a dog on a pork chop. They are engaged, full of energy, powerful, and positive—who wouldn't want to be around that?

Ask yourself, *How do I feel when a teammate or a coach acts enthusiastic on the bench?* Contrast that feeling with your experience of a teammate or coach who is dull, negative, or otherwise disengaged. Who would you rather be around? Enthusiasm injects a team with power and energy while a lack of enthusiasm feels like a black hole, draining the energy from everyone around it.

Enthusiasm is one of the few factors in hockey that can be ignited by one individual and quickly spread across the entire team, even an entire organization. Players wielding enthusiasm harness great power. Research tells us that in high-speed, high-pressure sports, it's not skill, knowledge, or experience, but the level of enthusiasm that has the greatest impact on the outcome. And one person can trigger this enthusiasm. What an awesome power!

Gratitude

In my experience as a hockey coach, hockey dad, and mental-game coach, one of the most overlooked tools we all have access to every day is an attitude of gratitude. Having gratitude for all the positive things in life doesn't cost money and doesn't take much time, but research shows that practicing gratitude increases grit, improves confidence, strengthens connection, and boosts your physical and mental health overall.

So, what is an attitude of gratitude? It's recognition for and appreciation of the positive aspects of yourself and others; it's a celebration of life in general. Think about how incredibly lucky you are to be healthy, fit, skilled, and athletic. You experience passion for a game you love so much and are around others who  support you and where you are going in life.

Playing hockey at the level you are playing is a privilege, to be sure. As you know, it takes a lot of time, money, effort, and support to make it all happen. Taking time each week to acknowledge what a wonderful opportunity you have been given will not only put you in sync with the universe, but it will also make you a better hockey player—a gritty, mentally tough, top-notch hockey player.

So, what are the specific benefits of practicing gratitude? Let's break them down. Grateful players experience fewer aches and pains and are generally healthier and less prone to injury. Gratitude improves your mental health as it reduces the frequency and intensity of negative emotions, such as anger, frustration, jealousy, resentment, and regret. Not only does it reduce negative emotions, but it also stimulates positive emotions, such as happiness, confidence, pride, and appreciation.

Research shows that grateful players actually sleep better after taking time to be thankful. Sleep is as important as nutrition and mental health, so improving the quality and quantity of your sleep through gratitude is an awesome benefit, indeed.

Gratitude also improves self-confidence and self-esteem. Earlier we talked about how critical confidence and self-esteem are in your hockey development and performance. Now research shows the simple act of gratitude can boost both of these.

An attitude of gratitude also increases mental toughness in hockey. When you take time to be grateful for all that you have, you become aware of your unique blessings and increase the purpose and passion you feel for the game and your life. And by now you know this all adds up to grit. In other words, gratitude increases grit. How cool is that?

So how do you intentionally increase the amount of gratitude you have in your game? Well, it's pretty simple, actually. The quickest and easiest way is to pick a time each week to sit for five minutes and make a list of the awesome things that happened to you for the week. Try to mix it up and avoid saying the same things over and over. Focus intently on all the amazing benefits you enjoy in life and jot them down.

Some people go all out, creating a gratitude journal and writing something in it every day. If that fits you, go for it. For many players I talk to, that would be too much and would turn them off to the exercise. So, find what works for you. Once a week, twice a week, five minutes, ten minutes, fifteen minutes—but do take the time to be thankful.

All of us have the ability to recognize and appreciate the gifts in our life. We all know that sometimes life can get intense. Things get hard and don't always go your way. Setbacks, adversity, and challenges are a reality in hockey. While gratitude won't eliminate these tough times, it does increase your resilience, restoring the passion and perseverance you need to move forward. Developing an attitude of gratitude is one of the simplest ways to improve your passion for and overall satisfaction in life.

Maintain Your Love for the Game

When you love hockey, all the sacrifices you make are worth the prize. Passion is an integral part of grit and you must maintain that passion to drive you forward, despite hardship and setbacks in your game. It's that relentless passion that gets you over the hump when circumstances make you weary, and you can use it as your touchstone to make sense of the world.

You started playing hockey and rose to your current level because you enjoyed the game. If that enjoyment is waning—for whatever reason—then it's time to assess your current level of passion.

To refresh and recapture your love of hockey, take a minute to remember what you loved about it when you were young. Clarify your goals and what you want to accomplish. The reality is that you will always be striving for the next level. The AA player is striving for AAA; the AAA player is striving for college or juniors; juniors and college players are striving for the pros, and the pros are striving to stay in the show.

The player with grit is *always* striving to reach the next level, and without passion and mental toughness to go along with elite physical skills, the journey can chew you up and spit you out. So, resolve to stay passionate and focused throughout your journey; this will maximize your effort on each rung of the ladder.

Conclusion

Grit is a blend of passion, perception, purpose, practice, and perseverance. Everyone who has achieved greatness made deliberate choices to move forward. Players who make it choose actions, thoughts, and a mindset that supports their goals. They choose to believe in themselves. And they choose to develop grit and mental toughness to move their game to the next level.

You don't have to be the biggest player on the ice. You don't have to be the smartest, the strongest, the fastest, or the one with the most natural gifts. Grit can level the playing field. Being gritty means you are not willing to compromise your goals or be content with mediocrity. In short, you are willing to work hard to become the best player you can be.

You have within you the power to achieve your maximum potential. Peak performance doesn't discriminate. If you strive for it, believe in it, and work toward it, you can become the player you want to be.

It starts with a choice, and the sooner you make it, the sooner your transformation begins.

Research shows that grit is a better predictor of success than any other factor. The ability to keep going despite setbacks is more important than your current skills, genetics, education, or environment.

Many talented players fall short because they simply give up; they refuse to stay the course when under pressure. As a player, you know it takes skill, talent, speed, strength, and fitness to play elite hockey. However, you must never forget the power that comes from developing your mental game. Being mentally tough isn't just something you do; it's who you are.

If you want to improve your hockey performance, take action now to increase the grit in your game. The next time you hear coaches say, "That player has grit" or "That kid shows great mental toughness," you'll know they're talking about you.

About the Complete Player Coaching Program

Now that you've read Hockey Grit, Grind, and Mind you know that grit is essential for elite play. Remember to take your free Grit Scale and HockeyType assessments at GritGrindMind.net.

But grit is just the beginning. Continue learning and growing with the Complete Player Mental Toughness Coaching Program. Visit us at GritGrindMind.net for FREE resources and coaching materials.

While you're there, check out all the resources offered at TheCompletePlayer.com, including courses, training, workbooks, workshops, webinars, seminars, team coaching, and individual coaching, all designed to make it easier for players to acquire and utilize the core mental toughness skills needed to play elite hockey. Together, Hockey Grit, Grind, and Mind and the Complete Player Mental Toughness Coaching Program provide essential mental coaching that, I believe, should be required for every player. That may sound boastful, but I have great confidence in the subject matter this material represents.

My mission is to help you develop the grit and toughness to take your game to the next level. I know this training works. I promise, if you'll dive into this training and use what you learn, you will become a better player.

If you have any questions or feedback, I'd love to hear from you. E-mail me at DrWillis@TCPhockey.com, or connect with me at Facebook, Twitter, and LinkedIn, and don't forget to get your free resources at GritGrindMind.net.

Notes

1. A. L. Duckworth, C. Peterson, M. D. Matthews, and D. R. Kelly, "Grit: Perseverance and Passion for Long-Term Goals," Journal of Personality and Social Psychology 9 (2007): 1087–1101.
2. A. L. Duckworth and P. D. Quinn, "Development and Validation of the Short Grit Scale (Grit- S)," Journal of Personality Assessment 91 (2009): 166–174.
3. R. M. Nideffer, Attentional Interpersonal Style Inventory. PsycTESTS Dataset. doi:10.1037/t05075-000.
4. M. Sagal, P. T. Sagal, and G. E. Miller, "Assessment in Sport Psychology," in Encyclopedia of Applied Psychology, ed. Charles Spielberger (Academic Press, 2004), 177–190. doi:10.1016/b0-12-657410-3/00799-6.
5. Saul L. Miller, Hockey Tough (Champaign, IL: Human Kinetics, 2016).
6. Daniel Coyle, The Talent Code: Greatness Isn't Born. It's Grown. Here's How (London: Arrow, 2010).
7. H. Weisinger and J. P. Pawliw-Fry, Performing under Pressure: The Science of Doing Your Best When It Matters Most (New York: Crown Publishing, 2015).

About the Author

Kevin Willis, Ph.D., is a performance and sport specialist consulting in sport and business and specializes in player psychological assessment for performing under pressure.

With a Ph.D. in sport psychology, Dr. Willis is one of North America's rising mental coaches in hockey. His work in enhancing performance and team building has helped hockey organizations, individuals, and teams be successful while dealing with pressure, stress, and change that comes with playing elite hockey.

Kevin has been working as a sport psychology consultant for 10 years mentored by Dr. Saul Miller, a leading mental game expert in the NHL for over 3 decades. Kevin has worked with elite teams from peewee to juniors and has helped hundreds of rising elite players strive towards their full potential.

Kevin is the founder of TheCompletePlayer.com and co-founder of HockeyTough.com and NetworkHockeyAdvisors.com and conducts seminars and workshops for teams, leagues, hockey organizations, coaching clinics, and conferences throughout North America.

Morgan James
Speakers Group

www.TheMorganJamesSpeakersGroup.com

We connect Morgan James published authors with live and online events and audiences who will benefit from their expertise.

Morgan James makes all of our titles available
through the Library for All Charity Organization.

www.LibraryForAll.org

CPSIA information can be obtained
at www.ICGtesting.com
Printed in the USA
BVHW03s1420190618
519427BV00002B/55/P